Gr. 1-4
TLC10588

100 M Little Reading Comprehension Lessons

Fun-to-read stories with skill-building exercises

Written by Margaret Brinton

Book Design by Patti Jeffers

Pick one... or pick a few.... these little lessons are... just for you!

Teaching and Learning Company
a Lorenz company
P.O. Box 802
Dayton, OH 45401-0802
www.LorenzEducationalPress.com

This book belongs to

_____

ISBN 978-1-4291-1830-9
Teaching and Learning Company,
a Lorenz company
P.O. Box 802
Dayton, OH 45401-0802
www.LorenzEducationalPress.com

Printed in the United States of America.

TLC10588

How to Use This Book

While working through the lessons in this book, students will build literacy and reading comprehension skills across a broad spectrum of genres and topics. *100 More Little Reading Comprehension Lessons* uses a combination of fiction, narrative, and poems to delight and entertain students. Non-fiction and fact-based prose are also included to expand knowledge and awareness of the world around us.

The comprehension questions following each passage are an important part of these lessons, and will allow students to practice and develop language arts skills while encouraging critical thinking and expression of opinion and thought.

As a teacher or parent, we suggest that you read each lesson aloud to students prior to their actually seeing the page. This will expand their auditory senses and awaken them to the pleasure of each story. Next, distribute the page and allow students to read the story silently and work through the comprehension questions and activities. You can conclude each lesson with an oral review of the story and comprehension questions and activities.

Reading is an entertaining and educational adventure for your students to experience! Embark on it!

Note: The bookmarks on page 4 can be reproduced, cut out, and distributed to students for in-class or independent reading.

Read pages ____ to ____ .
Write five new words here.

_____

_____

_____

_____

_____

Keep track of words you don't know. Look them up!

_____

_____

_____

_____

_____

Look for these words in your reading.

_____

_____

_____

_____

_____

I love to read! I have read these books.

_____

_____

_____

_____

_____

iv

Sweaters to Wear

All over the world, people wear sweaters. In very cold places, people wear heavy and warm sweaters. Those sweaters are sometimes itchy. They are itchy if they are made of wool. Wool is animal hair. That is why wool sweaters are very warm.

Some people do not need warm wool sweaters. They wear another kind of sweater made from cotton. A cotton sweater is soft and cool. Cotton comes from the fuzz of a special plant. Cotton is not made from animal hair.

In very cold places, people might wear a sweater under a jacket. In nice and warm places, they wear a sweater instead of a jacket. A sweater is a nice piece of clothing. It looks nice with pants or a skirt.

1. Why do some people need wool sweaters? _____

_____

_____

2. What three words describe wool sweaters? _____

_____

_____

3. For what is animal hair used? _____

_____

_____

4. Why is a cotton sweater soft? _____

_____

_____

5. What can a person wear with a sweater? _____

_____

_____

6. On your own paper, draw and color your favorite sweater.

Name _____

Non-fiction

A Lot to Learn About Owls

An owl is a very skilled hunter. That is why it is called a *bird of prey*. Some owls hunt for rabbits. Other owls hunt for rodents such as rats or mice. Some owls prefer to catch frogs or toads.

An owl is a good hunter because it has large eyes. Those large eyes are very sharp. They help owls search for food. An owl also has good ears that listen for other animal sounds. It can attack quickly and trap another animal. It traps with its sharp claws.

Most owls live and nest in a tree. A few owls will live in another animal's tunnel. Other owls choose a barn on a farm for nesting. Farmers like to have owls because owls eat the rats. Owls snatch rats with their claws.

1. Find out what "bird of prey" means. _____

_____

_____

2. Name three things an owl hunts besides rodents

_____

_____

3. What two words describe an owl's eyes?

_____

_____

4. What can an owl do with its claws? _____

_____

_____

5. What does an owl sometimes borrow? _____

_____

_____

6. Why do many owls like to live in the forest? _____

_____

_____

6

TLC10588

What to Do with Carrots

Carrots are wonderful vegetables. Carrots are full of vitamins. They also have a lot of fiber. Fiber helps your body digest other foods, such as meat. Other vegetables besides carrots have fiber.

Children often eat crunchy, raw carrots. Carrots do not need to be cooked. They are delicious when they are cooked. Parents often cook carrots in a soup. It is also healthy to boil carrots and then bake them into a cake. Other people enjoy carrot muffins. Did you ever hear of a carrot pie?

When children play in the snow, they sometimes use carrots. They can stick a fresh, raw carrot into a snowman's face. That carrot becomes the snowman's bright, orange nose!

1. Name two reasons why carrots are good for your health.

_____

_____

2. How can carrots be fun for children? _____

_____

_____

3. When do people boil carrots? _____

_____

_____

4. Why don't people use a cooked carrot for a snowman's nose? _____

_____

_____

5. Why are carrots a quick snack? _____

_____

_____

6. What are two things we can do to help our bodies digest meat?

_____

_____

Have a Picnic

Some families like to eat lunch outdoors. Eating lunch outdoors is called a *picnic*. It is fun to have a picnic on a sunny day. It is also nice to have a picnic on a cool, fall day. It is NOT enjoyable to have a picnic in the rain. Would anyone plan a picnic in the snow?

Many places are good places to have a picnic. People who live in an apartment go to a city park for a picnic. People who live in a house plan a picnic in their backyard. A farm family can have a picnic in the field. Another fun place for a picnic is by the water. A family can put a blanket on the beach for their picnic. Some people even eat a picnic lunch in a boat! A picnic lunch tastes good outdoors!

1. In this story, what are some good places for a picnic?

_____

_____

2. Think of two other good places for a picnic.

_____

_____

3. Why would a picnic in a farm field be interesting? _____

_____

_____

4. Why would a picnic at the beach be fun? _____

_____

_____

5. In what weather do people NOT have a picnic? _____

_____

_____

6. What kind of sandwich would you like for your picnic? _____

_____

_____

The Largest Bird

The biggest bird in the world is the ostrich. The ostrich is very large, but its wings are small. That's why the ostrich can never get off the ground. The wings are just too little. The ostrich can run fast, but it cannot fly. Its strong legs can run and kick.

The ostrich is taller than a man. It is also heavier than most people. This huge bird can weigh 300 pounds! That is why the ostrich lays very large eggs. Their nests are giant holes in the sand! The male helps to keep the eggs warm. After a while, the eggs hatch. Each new chick is a young ostrich.

1. What four words tell you that the ostrich is big? _____

_____

_____

2. What kind of nest does the ostrich have? _____

_____

_____

3. Why is the nest so large? _____

_____

_____

4. Why is the ostrich a strange bird? _____

_____

_____

5. Why doesn't the ostrich need to fly? _____

_____

_____

6. How can the ostrich fight an enemy? _____

_____

_____

Happy by the Lake

Jenny enjoys sitting on a bench by the lake. She and her brother sit on that bench and they talk. Jenny and her brother talk about the duck that swims in the lake. They talk about the white goose that stands on the shore.

A large tree gives shade to that bench by the lake. Jenny and her brother look up at the tree. A bluebird with a rusty-orange chest sits upon a branch. A pine cone drops from the tree and rolls under the bench. Jenny's brother picks up the pine cone. It is sticky from the sap of the tree.

Soon, a frog jumps past the bench. That frog has just caught a fly on its sticky tongue! Jenny and her brother have a good laugh about that. They are happy on the bench by the lake.

1. Why is it nice and cool where Jenny and her brother sit?

_____

_____

2. What three birds do they notice? _____

_____

_____

3. Which bird is the most active? _____

_____

_____

4. Why was it easy to spot the bluebird? _____

_____

_____

5. What are two sticky things in this story? _____

_____

_____

6. What did Jenny and her brother do together besides watch the animals?

_____

About a Snake

A snake is a creature that slides,
Through grasses a slender snake glides.
It moves through the dirt,
It doesn't get hurt.
Down in a hole the snake hides.

1. What two words rhyme with "slides?"

   _____

   _____

2. What word means the same as "slides?" _____

   _____

   _____

3. Where does the snake go? _____

   _____

   _____

4. What does the word "slender" mean? _____

   _____

   _____

5. Copy this poem on your own paper.

6. Try to memorize this poem.

In Their Sailboat

Anne and Joel are getting ready. They will go with their parents in their sailboat today. Anne and Joel each have a beach bag. They pack their own beach bag to go sailing. Anne packs lip gloss, books, and a small radio. Joel puts toy trucks and a hat in his beach bag.

Ann and Joel walk to the end of the boat dock. Their parents help them get safely into their boat. Mother snaps the buckles on their life jackets. Then, Father unties the boat's ropes from the dock.

The summer breeze blows against the boat's sails. The sails puff up with the gentle wind, and the boat moves away from the dock. Father steers the boat across the lake. The summer sun is hot, but the wind across the water is cool. It is a wonderful sailing day!

1. What three things will Anne do on the boat?

_____

_____

2. What will Joel do on the boat? _____

_____

_____

3. Where does the family get on their boat? _____

_____

_____

4. When does father untie the ropes? _____

_____

_____

5. Name two reasons why it is a great day for sailing. _____

_____

_____

6. How does the boat get across the lake? _____

_____

The Work of a Leaf

A leaf on a tree or plant is pretty to see. A red or orange autumn leaf on the ground has natural beauty. But a leaf is more than just a pretty thing. A leaf has a job to do. A leaf must make food to feed the tree!

How does a simple, green leaf make food for the tree? First, each green leaf on a tree collects the light and heat from the sun. Then, each leaf collects the fresh air. The leaf uses the carbon dioxide in the air. The leaf also collects water. The water comes into the tree through the roots. The water comes up to the leaves. With light, heat, air, and water, the leaf can work. The leaf changes everything into sugar. That sugar will keep the tree or plant alive!

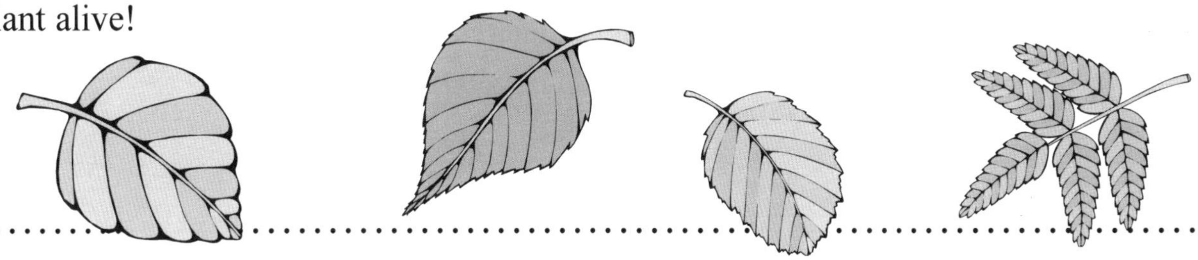

1. Why do people like leaves? _____

_____

_____

2. Why do trees need leaves? _____

_____

_____

3. What six words describe leaves in this story? _____

_____

_____

4. What two things does a leaf need from the sun? _____

_____

5. What does a leaf need from underground? _____

_____

_____

6. Why don't trees get much sugar in the autumn? _____

_____

_____

Take Time for Music

Music is something very nice for our health. It is good to take time for music each day. Music helps a person's mind relax. Music will even help our brains think better. Music helps us organize our brain!

A person can make music by singing. A person can also hum a little tune. Some people like to whistle a song. It is also possible to snap your fingers to make a musical beat. Other people tap their feet to create a beat or rhythm.

It is also good to listen to music on the radio. Some people use a CD player to listen to music. Other people go to a parade to hear a band playing music. Others like to listen to a musical concert on stage. In every case, music is good for a person's health.

1. What are three ways to make your own musical song?

   _____

   _____

   _____

2. What are two ways to make your own musical beat?

   _____

   _____

3. Where can you hear good music? _____

   _____

   _____

4. How does good music help your mind? _____

   _____

   _____

5. How might good music help organize your brain? _____

   _____

   _____

6. Try to sing or hum your own little song.

14

A Lot of Life

A rain forest is a very damp place. So much rain falls that the air there is always moist. Trees and plants and vines grow very well in a rain forest. A rain forest is thick with leaves and branches, too.

Thousands of colorful birds sing in a rain forest. Thousands of small animals run up and down the tree trunks. Other animals swing from vine to vine. A rain forest is a very busy place. Insects chew through the leaves. Spiders spin beautiful webs. Some animals work together as a team. Other animals eat each other up!

A river often flows through a rain forest. A river is full of life. Fish, eels, turtles, and crocodiles swim there. A rain forest has creatures everywhere!

1. What two words in the story mean "wet?" _____

_____

2. What are seven creatures in this story? _____

_____

_____

3. What are eight actions of all these creatures? _____

_____

_____

4. Why are there so many leaves in a rain forest? _____

_____

5. Why are the leaves so important? _____

_____

_____

6. Why do the creatures stay healthy in a rain forest? _____

_____

_____

7. On your own paper, draw a colorful picture of this story.

So Many Books

Aren't books wonderful? Books are full of ideas! A person can always learn new things from a book. A book gives a person something new to think about.

If you look at an art book, you will learn about colors. You will also learn about style and design. If you read a storybook, you will learn about a character. A storybook is a book of fiction. A fiction book has made-up characters. It has a made-up story, too.

In a nonfiction book, everything is true. Some nonfiction books tell about famous people. Other nonfiction books explain animal life. School books, such as science books, are also nonfiction. Most people read both fiction and nonfiction books.

1. How do people get a lot of new ideas? _____

_____

_____

2. Name two things you can learn from an art book.

_____

_____

3. What is not true in a storybook? _____

_____

_____

4. Is a biography a book of fiction or nonfiction? _____

_____

_____

5. What kinds of books give you facts instead of fiction? _____

_____

_____

6. What are the titles of three books that you like?

_____

_____

_____

TLC10588

Around North America

North America is a large continent. North America has three main countries. Those countries are Canada, Mexico, and the United States. There are also some small parts called Latin America.

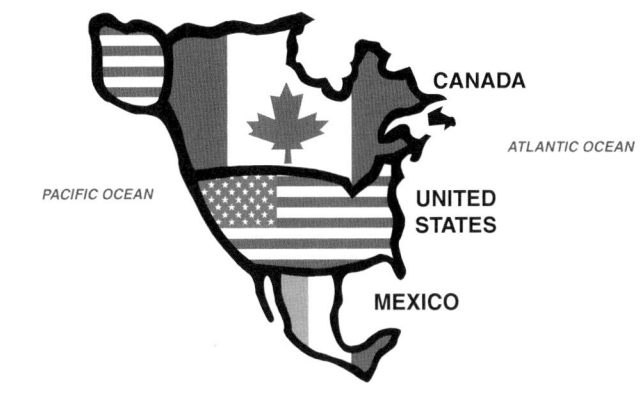

To the west of North America is the Pacific Ocean. The beaches there are on the Pacific Coast. Those beaches go for thousands of miles.

To the east of North America is the Atlantic Ocean. The beaches there are on the Atlantic Coast. Those beaches also go for thousands of miles.

So, you see, between the Pacific Ocean and the Atlantic Ocean is a continent. That continent is North America. There is a coast on each side.

1. On what continent do you live? _____

_____

_____

2. In what country do you live? _____

_____

_____

3. On what continent is the country of Mexico? _____

_____

_____

4. Why do people like to go to the Pacific Coast? _____

_____

_____

5. Why do people like to go to the Atlantic Coast? _____

_____

_____

6. What is to the west of the United States? _____

_____

Fun at the Beach

Jack and Jake sit in the sand by the sea. They are brothers and their hobby is to make sand castles. Their sand castles are large and artistic. People walking by often stop and stare at the castles. They ask Jack and Jake how they do this.

Jack and Jake explain how to make sand castles. They say it is important to pack many buckets full of sand. After that, they pile up more and more sand. Jack and Jake explain how to pack the loose sand together. Then, it is time to shape the sand castle. Shovels and scrapers are good, flat tools for that. To shape and scrape the sand castle is never easy. But because it is their hobby, Jack and Jake like to do it!

. . . .

1. Why do Jack and Jake need to be a good team? _____

_____

_____

2. Do you think making sand castles is work or play for them? Explain. _____

_____

_____

3. Why do other people notice their castles? _____

_____

_____

4. Why do they need so many buckets of sand? _____

_____

_____

5. Why is it important to pack the sand after they dump it out? _____

_____

_____

6. How do they give shape to their castles? _____

_____

_____

Name _____

All about Fish

Fish live in waters all over the world. Some fish live in the ocean. Fish in any ocean are called *saltwater* fish. Another type of fish is the *freshwater* fish. Freshwater fish do not live in the oceans of the world. They live in ponds, lakes, or rivers.

Some saltwater fish are sharks. Other saltwater fish are stingrays. The flying fish also lives in the ocean. So does the tuna and the eel.

Some freshwater fish are trout. Trout often live in streams in the mountains. Some fish in a lake are little perch. In a deep river, there are freshwater fish called *catfish*. Other freshwater fish are pike. Freshwater fish cannot survive in the ocean, and saltwater fish cannot live in a pond.

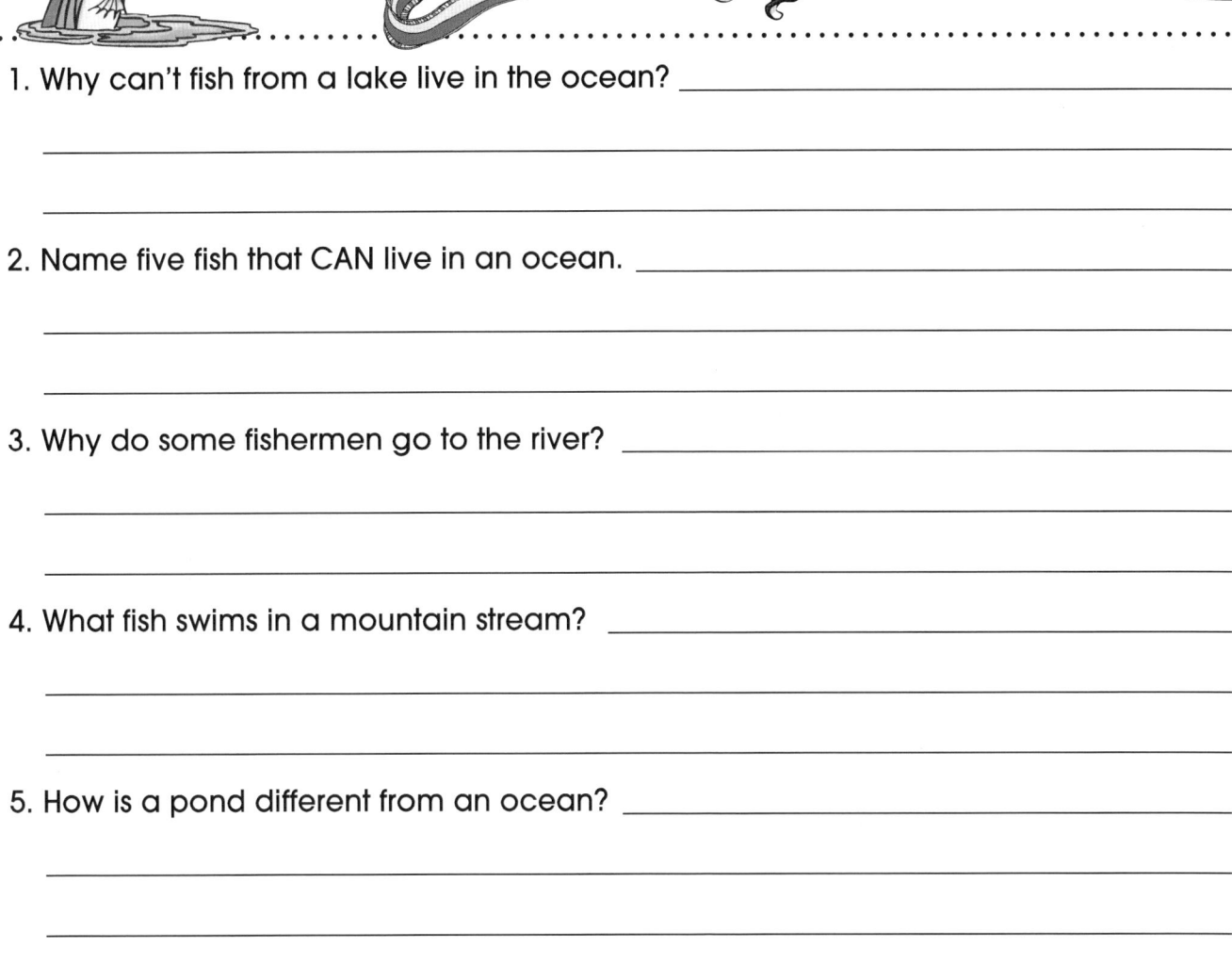

1. Why can't fish from a lake live in the ocean? _____

_____

_____

2. Name five fish that CAN live in an ocean. _____

_____

_____

3. Why do some fishermen go to the river? _____

_____

_____

4. What fish swims in a mountain stream? _____

_____

_____

5. How is a pond different from an ocean? _____

_____

_____

6. Why do some ocean fishermen have to be brave and strong? _____

_____

_____

Music in Nature

Music is something beautiful for our ears to hear. We can hear music in many ways. Did you know we can hear music in nature? When you go outside, listen carefully. Listen to the sounds of nature.

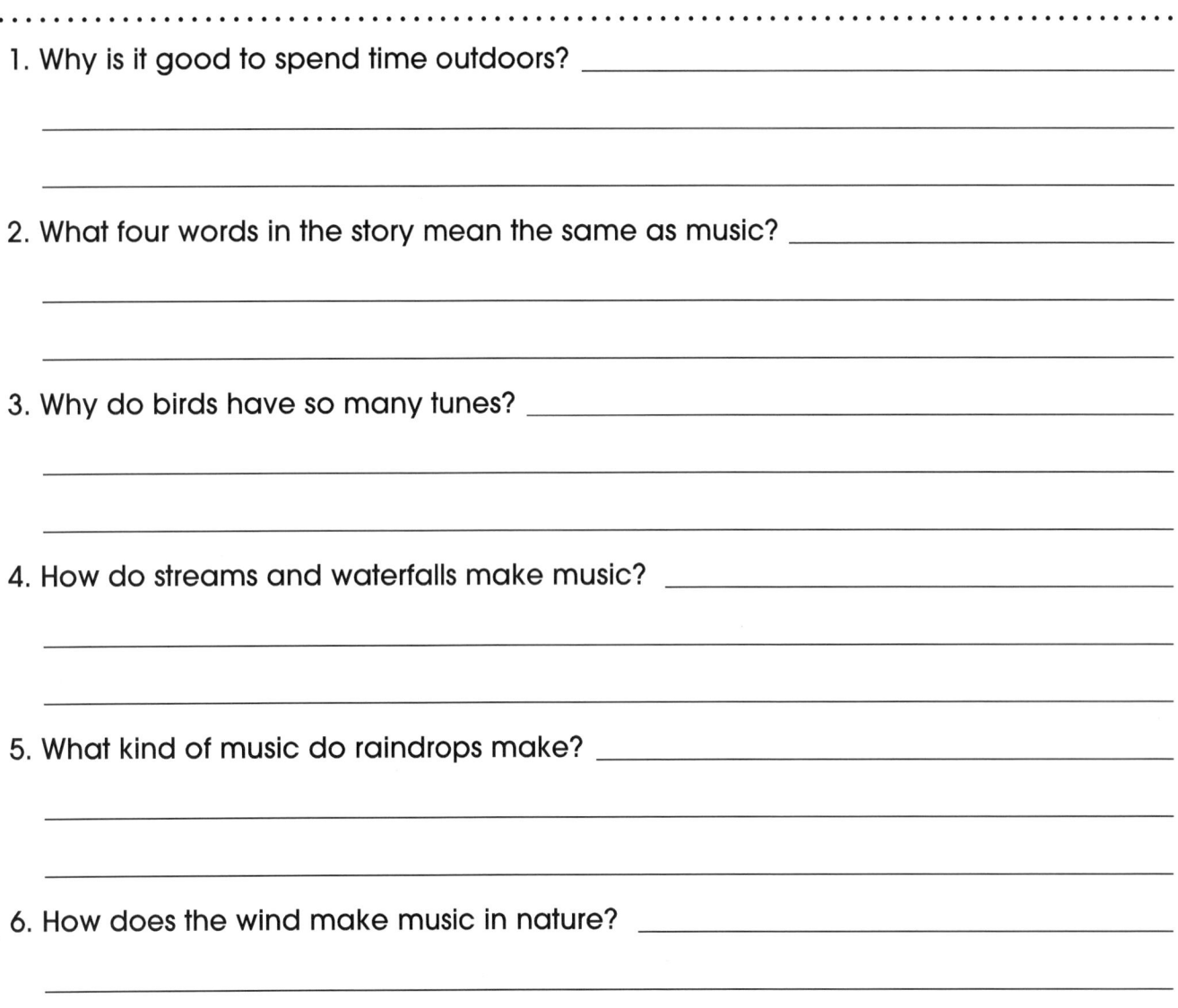

Birds sing and chirp. The sound from a bird is music to our ears. Each kind of bird sings its own tune. Those tunes are nature's music. The tune of a bird is a song.

We can also hear beautiful music in water. If you listen to a waterfall flowing down, that is music. Take time to listen to a stream flowing along. The water moving in a stream makes music. Even the leaves make music on a windy day. Splashing raindrops make music, too! Just listen to nature's music.

1. Why is it good to spend time outdoors? _____

_____

_____

2. What four words in the story mean the same as music? _____

_____

_____

3. Why do birds have so many tunes? _____

_____

_____

4. How do streams and waterfalls make music? _____

_____

_____

5. What kind of music do raindrops make? _____

_____

_____

6. How does the wind make music in nature? _____

_____

_____

Different Kinds of Gardens

People who live in a house sometimes have a garden. A garden is a place to plant seeds. With good dirt and enough water and sunshine, the seeds will grow. Some seeds grow into bright flowers. Other seeds grow into fruit or vegetable plants.

Some people do not want to grow flowers or vegetables. People may want to have a rock garden instead. In a rock garden, there are pretty stones and nice, fresh dirt. People can put sticks or shells in a rock garden, too.

For people in apartments, there is another kind of garden. This kind of garden is in a wooden box. The wooden box is built under a window. People plant small flowers in this box. This garden is called a *window box*. It is not in the ground.

1. What three kinds of seeds do people plant? _____

_____

_____

2. What kind of garden is in an apartment? _____

_____

_____

3. In what kind of ground do seeds grow well? _____

_____

4. How can you decorate a rock garden? _____

_____

_____

5. Why would a window box be exciting? _____

_____

_____

6. Why do you think a rock garden is called a "garden?" _____

_____

A Frog or a Toad?

A frog and a toad are both amphibians. As amphibians, they spend time on land and in water. A frog and a toad both lay eggs. When they hatch, tadpoles swim around like little fish. After a while, their legs and feet develop. Now, the tadpole has become a frog or a toad, and it can jump!

A frog and a toad are not exactly the same. The skin of a frog is usually smooth. The toad's skin is bumpy. A frog's body is long when it jumps or leaps. A toad's body is fat and chunky.

A frog spends a lot of time in a lake or pond. A toad likes to sit on the ground and wait for bugs to pass by. In winter, both a frog and a toad live under the mud! It is nice and warm under the mud.

1. Where do amphibians live? _____

_____

_____

2. Why is a tadpole NOT an amphibian? _____

_____

_____

3. When does a tadpole change into a frog or toad? _____

_____

_____

4. Why doesn't a toad look smooth like a frog? _____

_____

_____

5. What is another word for "fat" in this story? _____

_____

6. When does a frog stretch out its body? _____

_____

7. Why don't frogs and toads mind the cold winters? _____

Some Very Deep Lakes

A "great" lake means a very large lake. North America has five Great Lakes. The five Great Lakes are large and deep. They are deep enough for very big ships.

The Great Lakes are between Canada and the United States. The names of the lakes are Superior, Michigan, Huron, Erie, and Ontario. These lakes all connect to each other through rivers and canals.

Ships from all over the world can sail on the Great Lakes. First, these ships travel on the Atlantic Ocean. They carry heavy loads of boxes and freight. From the Atlantic Ocean, the ships enter a deep river. This river connects to the Great Lakes. The ships continue to travel. Around the Great Lakes are cities called *ports*. The ships deliver their boxes and freight at these ports. Then the ships sail back to the ocean.

1. What are the three jobs of the ships in this story? _____

_____

_____

2. What are "ports?" _____

_____

_____

3. Why are ports important in this story? _____

_____

_____

4. How do the ships get from the ocean to the Great Lakes? _____

_____

_____

5. How can these ships get from one lake to another lake? _____

_____

_____

6. Name the five Great Lakes. _____

_____

A Bad Snake to Be Around

Some people like snakes. Other people dislike them. One snake that most people don't like is the rattlesnake. There is a reason to fear a rattlesnake. It has venom in its bite. The venom is a poison, and a person can die from it.

Some people go walking in areas where rattlesnakes live. These people are called *hikers*. When they hike, they are careful about each step. They do not step close to large rocks or logs. That is where rattlesnakes hide.

A rattlesnake has little, bony rings on its tail. A rattlesnake will lift up its tail and shake it. That shake is called a rattle. Now, the snake is ready to attack. A hiker must always be aware!

· ·

1. What do you think "dislike" means? _____

_____

_____

2. What word in this story means "be careful?" _____

_____

_____

3. Name four reasons why hikers fear rattlesnakes. _____

_____

_____

4. From where does venom come? _____

_____

_____

5. How can a rattlesnake make a "rattle" sound? _____

_____

_____

6. Why might a hiker not see a rattlesnake? _____

_____

TLC10588

What is Silver?

A person can wear a ring made of silver. They can also put a silver necklace around their neck. A person might put a silver pin on a coat. Silver jewelry is pretty because it shines. That makes people want to have silver.

Silver is a very shiny metal. Miners have to dig to find it. They usually do not find a solid piece of silver. They find a rocky area with metal in the rock. The metal might be silver. It could also be a different metal. The rock with the metal is called *ore*. There is a way to get the silver out of the ore. Silver is then made into jewelry. Coins and bells and belt buckles are also made from silver.

1. What are six things that are made from silver? _____

_____

_____

2. Why do people like to have silver? _____

_____

_____

3. Where do miners find silver? _____

_____

_____

4. Why do miners dig for ore? _____

_____

_____

5. Where do miners dig for ore? _____

_____

_____

6. Name two reasons why miners sell the silver when they find it. _____

_____

_____

Going to the Mountains

Jan and Jon are twins. They live with their mom and dad. They live in a town that never gets cold. The town never has snow in the winter. But they can see the mountains in the distance and the mountains have snow.

Sometimes, the twins' parents take them to the mountains. Everyone puts on a heavy jacket. They all wear fuzzy mittens on their hands. They each have a warm, winter cap.

The family enjoys playing in the snow. They make a huge circle like a track in the snow. That circle is like a track. They chase each other around the track. They slip. They slide. They get wet when they fall down, but that snow play is fun!

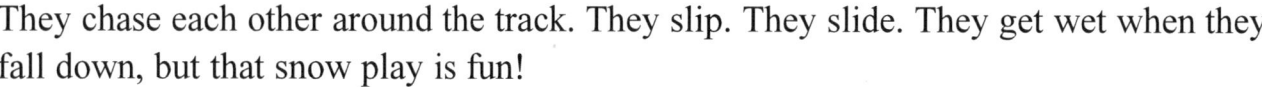

1. Why would Jan and Jon look far away to the mountains? _____

_____

_____

2. How far away are the mountains? _____

_____

_____

3. How does the family prepare for snow play? _____

_____

_____

4. Name six things the family does in the snow. _____

_____

_____

5. When might Jan and Jon lose their caps? _____

_____

_____

6. Why does their track need to be huge? _____

_____

26

How People Use Oil

People use oil in many different ways. There is not just one kind of oil that people use. Every oil has a different purpose.

One kind of oil comes from deep in the earth. That kind of oil is deep in the land or the sea. Special machines have to drill to get the oil out. They drill into the ground or into the sea floor. This kind of oil is what people put into their car's engine. Truck engines need this oil, too. It helps the engines work smoothly.

Another kind of oil comes from food. Peanuts have oil. Olives have oil, too. Corn and soy beans also have oil. People use oil from these plant foods to cook other foods.

There is also oil in animals. Whales and seals have oil in their bodies. That kind of oil is used to make soap and candles. Long ago, that oil was used to light a lamp or a lantern.

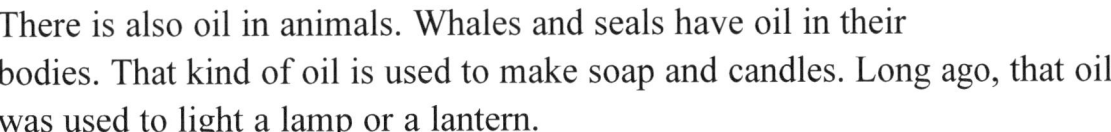

1. Why do so many machines drill for oil? _____

_____

_____

2. From where does the oil for engines come? _____

_____

3. Why do some people use peanut oil? _____

_____

_____

4. What three oils are used for cooking? _____

_____

_____

5. From what are some candles and soaps made? _____

_____

_____

6. Why don't people need so much seal or whale oil today? _____

_____

The Dangers of Oceans

The west coast of America meets the Pacific Ocean. On America's east coast is the Atlantic Ocean. A coast is where the land stops and the ocean begins.

An ocean can be a dangerous body of water. It can be dangerous for swimmers and for surfers. An ocean is not safe for small boats, either. Even large ships have accidents. But ocean animals are safe in the water.

The deepness of an ocean is one great danger. Large, stormy winds are another problem. Other dangers are caused by the currents. The powerful currents are rivers of water in an ocean.

. . . .

1. What two oceans are named in this story? _____

_____

_____

2. In this story, what are the three things that make an ocean dangerous?

_____

_____

3. Why don't sea animals worry about the ocean? _____

_____

_____

4. What might not be safe in an ocean? _____

_____

_____

5. What is a river that flows in an ocean called? _____

_____

_____

TLC10588

Millions of Years Ago

Different animals lived millions of years ago. Some of those animals were dinosaurs. They have been extinct for a long time. That means that dinosaurs do not live anymore.

Some people have found dinosaur bones while digging in the ground. Scientists put these bones back together to make a dinosaur skeleton. That is how we can know what some dinosaurs looked like.

One kind of dinosaur had feet like a giant bird. Another dinosaur had a little head on its very long neck. One type of dinosaur had sharp spikes on its tail. Another dinosaur's long tail stuck up in the air. One dinosaur was called *T-REX*. T-REX was huge, and his claws were eight inches long!

. . . .

1. Why can't we go to a zoo to see a dinosaur? _____

_____

2. Why did T-REX look so fierce? _____

_____

_____

3. What is silly about some dinosaurs' tails? _____

_____

_____

4. Why could one dinosaur attack with its tail? _____

_____

_____

5. How do some people know what dinosaurs looked like? _____

_____

_____

6. Why are old dinosaur bones important? _____

_____

_____

7. Draw a dinosaur on your own paper.

Lots of Shaking

Volcanoes are something to fear.

Their rumbles are not good to hear.

The large mountain shakes,

The low valley quakes.

Let's hope it won't happen this year!

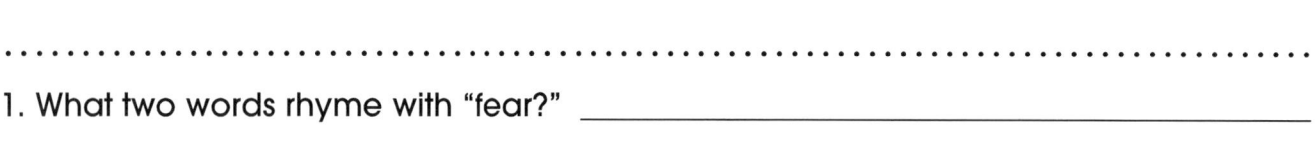

1. What two words rhyme with "fear?" _____

   _____

   _____

2. What is the sound of a volcano? _____

   _____

   _____

3. When does a volcano rumble? _____

   _____

   _____

4. What does "quake" mean? _____

   _____

   _____

5. Copy this poem on your own paper.

6. Try to memorize this poem.

TLC10588

How People Feel

Your feelings are part of your health. Your feelings are called *emotions*.

One kind of feeling is anger. Anger is when you feel mad about something. Too much anger can lead to hate. Hate is a very bad emotion to feel. When you start to feel angry, try to calm down.

Another feeling is sadness. You might feel sad for a good reason. Many sad things happen in life. Try to tell someone why you are sad. Then look for reasons to feel better.

Another feeling is happiness. Happiness is a healthy emotion. If you feel happy, your body is stronger. Try to have a smile on your face. Look for good things to laugh about. Show kindness to other people. It is healthy to have joy.

1. What are the three main emotions in this story? _____

_____

_____

2. Why is happiness a healthy emotion? _____

_____

_____

3. Why should you control your anger? _____

_____

_____

4. What are two things you can do about sadness? _____

_____

_____

5. From where does joy come? _____

_____

_____

6. Why is it good to smile every day? _____

_____

_____

Kids Go Surfing

Surfers go surfing in the ocean. A surfer rides a surfboard on the waves. Many boys and girls learn to surf.

Kids can learn to surf at an early age. They must first know how to swim very well. The ocean is dangerous. A surfer must be a strong swimmer.

Surfers learn to carry their surfboards into the water. When the water gets deep, they lie down on their boards. They use their arms to paddle. They paddle out to the waves. Then they wait on their boards. They wait for the best wave to come. When they see a good wave, they get up on their knees. Then they stand on their boards. They must balance very well.

. . . .

1. Why must any surfer be strong? _____

_____

_____

2. Name two places where surfers go to surf. _____

_____

_____

3. For what do all surfers wait? _____

_____

_____

4. Why is the ocean dangerous? _____

_____

_____

5. Why does a surfer need strong arms? _____

_____

_____

6. Why does a surfer need strong legs? _____

_____

_____

TLC10588

One Strange Creature

Eddy's father swims and dives in the ocean. He tells Eddy about his adventures in the water. He also talks about one great danger there. That danger is the octopus. The octopus can be a serious threat.

Eddy's father knows a lot about the octopus. He knows he must always avoid them. A large octopus in the ocean can kill a human. It has eight long arms. Those arms can trap a person and squeeze.

Eddy's father says that an octopus looks strange because it has so many arms. And the arms come out from the head! There is something else strange about an octopus. An octopus can change the color of its own body. That way it can fool its enemies.

· ·

1. How does Eddy's father know so much about the ocean? _____

_____

_____

2. What does "avoid" the octopus mean? _____

_____

_____

3. Name three reasons why the arms of an octopus are a danger to a human.

_____

_____

4. What are three very strange things about the octopus? _____

_____

_____

5. Why might a shark not see an octopus? _____

_____

_____

6. Why is the octopus a serious threat? _____

_____

_____

A School Report

Rico was born in Kansas. In second grade, he did a report about his state. His Aunt Tina helped him with the report. Aunt Tina told him all about the state where he was born.

Rico learned that Kansas is quite a flat state. There are a few hills, but there are no mountains. Some high, rocky areas are near a river. Those high areas of rock are called *bluffs*. Kansas also has dozens of deep lakes. Those lakes hold a large supply of fresh water.

To complete his report, Rico needed more facts. Aunt Tina told him that much of Kansas is grassland. The ranchers send their cows to eat in the grassland. Aunt Tina also told Rico about the wheat farms. The farmers grow tons of wheat. The wheat from Kansas is made into bread and cereal.

. . . .

1. Why is Aunt Tina important in this story? _____

_____

_____

2. What do we call the true information in any report? _____

_____

_____

3. Name two places where a person could go climbing in Kansas.

_____

_____

4. Where could a person catch fish in Kansas? _____

_____

_____

5. Name four reasons why Kansas needs a lot of rain. _____

_____

_____

6. Why is Kansas important for all of us? _____

_____

_____

Around the Sun

The moon and the earth have some fun.

Together they orbit the sun.

They make a round trip,

They don't lose their grip.

A new year begins when they're done.

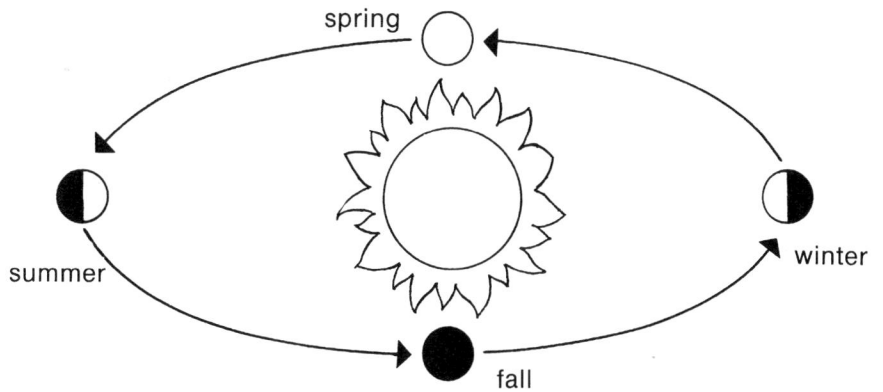

1. What two words rhyme with "fun"? _____

_____

_____

2. Why do the moon and the earth need a kind of grip? _____

_____

_____

3. How long does it take them to orbit the sun? _____

_____

_____

4. What idea in the poem makes the moon and the earth like characters?

_____

_____

5. Copy this poem on your own paper.

6. Try to memorize this poem.

What is Leather?

One day, Casey talked to his grandfather. He wanted to learn about his grandfather's life. He asked about his grandfather's work. He learned that his grandfather worked with leather. He learned that leather is the skin of an animal. He found out that humans have many uses for leather.

Casey's grandfather worked in a leather factory. He worked with the skins of goats and cows. He also worked with the skins of pigs, deer, and lizards. Casey's grandfather knew how to cut and shape the skins. He could also stitch and sew the leather pieces together.

Casey learned even more about leather. His grandfather told him that shoes are made from leather. Boots, belts and even winter gloves are made from leather. Long ago, people made pants and shirts from leather. The skin of a deer is a nice, soft leather for pants and shirts.

1. With what material did Casey's grandfather work? _____

_____

_____

2. From what five animals does leather come? _____

_____

_____

3. What did Casey's grandfather do in the factory? _____

_____

_____

4. For what three things would the strongest leather be used? _____

_____

_____

5. For what was the softest leather used? _____

_____

_____

Our Country's Parks

Most towns have a park. Big cities have many parks. A park is a place to enjoy nature. People can relax in a park and children can play there.

The biggest parks are called *national parks*. A national park is not in a town or city. A national park is in the middle of nature away from where people live. The word "national" means "about our country." America has many national parks.

Wild alligators live in one national park. That park is in the state of Florida. Huge creatures called buffalo live in a national park in Wyoming. A national park in Hawaii has volcanoes. The largest trees in the world grow in a national park, too. That park is in the state of California.

1. Name three reasons why people like city parks. _____

_____

_____

2. Why are national parks away from the city? _____

_____

_____

3. About what country is the story? _____

_____

_____

4. What are the four states in this story? _____

_____

_____

5. Why must people be careful in Wyoming's national park? _____

_____

_____

6. When would Hawaii's national park be dangerous? _____

_____

_____

At the Lakeshore

Some families like to spend time at a lake. They sit and play on the sand by the lake. That sand is called the *lakeshore*. The lakeshore is a kind of beach.

One family might eat a picnic lunch on a blanket at the lakeshore. Another family might go there to build a sand castle. Some families are at the lakeshore to go fishing. Others are there to sail toy boats in the water. Some families have their own big boat to sail.

The lakeshore is a busy place in the summer. Children swim along the shore. Other children float on large, plastic water toys. The lake feels cool and fresh. The sand is warm. For those reasons, families visit the lakeshore.

1. What is the sandy beach in this story called? _____

_____

_____

2. Name three ways people might cool off on a summer day at the lake.

_____

_____

3. How could a person warm up after swimming? _____

_____

_____

4. What are four other activities you can do at the lakeshore? _____

_____

_____

5. Which kind of fun do you think has the most adventure? _____

_____

_____

6. Why do some people put down a blanket at the lakeshore? _____

_____

_____

TLC10588

Eating the Right Kinds of Food

Children enjoy munching on cookies. Children also like to crunch on salty chips. And, of course, eating chewy candy is fun! Cookies and chips and candy are treats, however. They are not healthy foods for your body.

To be able to grow strong, children need to eat right. Children need milk and other dairy foods like yogurt and cheese. Children need bread and other grains like cereal. Meat, fish, and eggs are also very important foods. Some of the best foods are vegetables. Another great food group is fruit. Nuts are healthy, too.

Children need to eat many pieces of vegetables and fruit every day. Fruit needs to be washed. It does not need to be cooked. Some vegetables can be eaten raw, too. Some delicious raw vegetables are carrots, lettuce, and celery. You only need to rinse the raw vegetables in fresh water before eating them.

. . . .

1. What are two words that mean "eat" in this story? _____

_____

_____

2. How are treats different from real food? _____

_____

_____

3. What are three dairy foods in this story? _____

_____

_____

4. Name eight other good foods in this story. _____

_____

_____

5. Why is salad quick and easy to make? _____

_____

_____

Watching Birds

Father took Becky to the beach. They did not go to the beach to swim. They did not go to dig in the sand. They went to the beach to watch for birds! Father was writing a book about birds. He needed to learn more about them for his book.

Father and Becky watched a little plover. The plover was pecking at a seashell. The plover tried to get a snail out of the seashell. Another bird was called a turnstone. The turnstone was hunting for crabs near the rocks. It turned stones over to find clams to eat.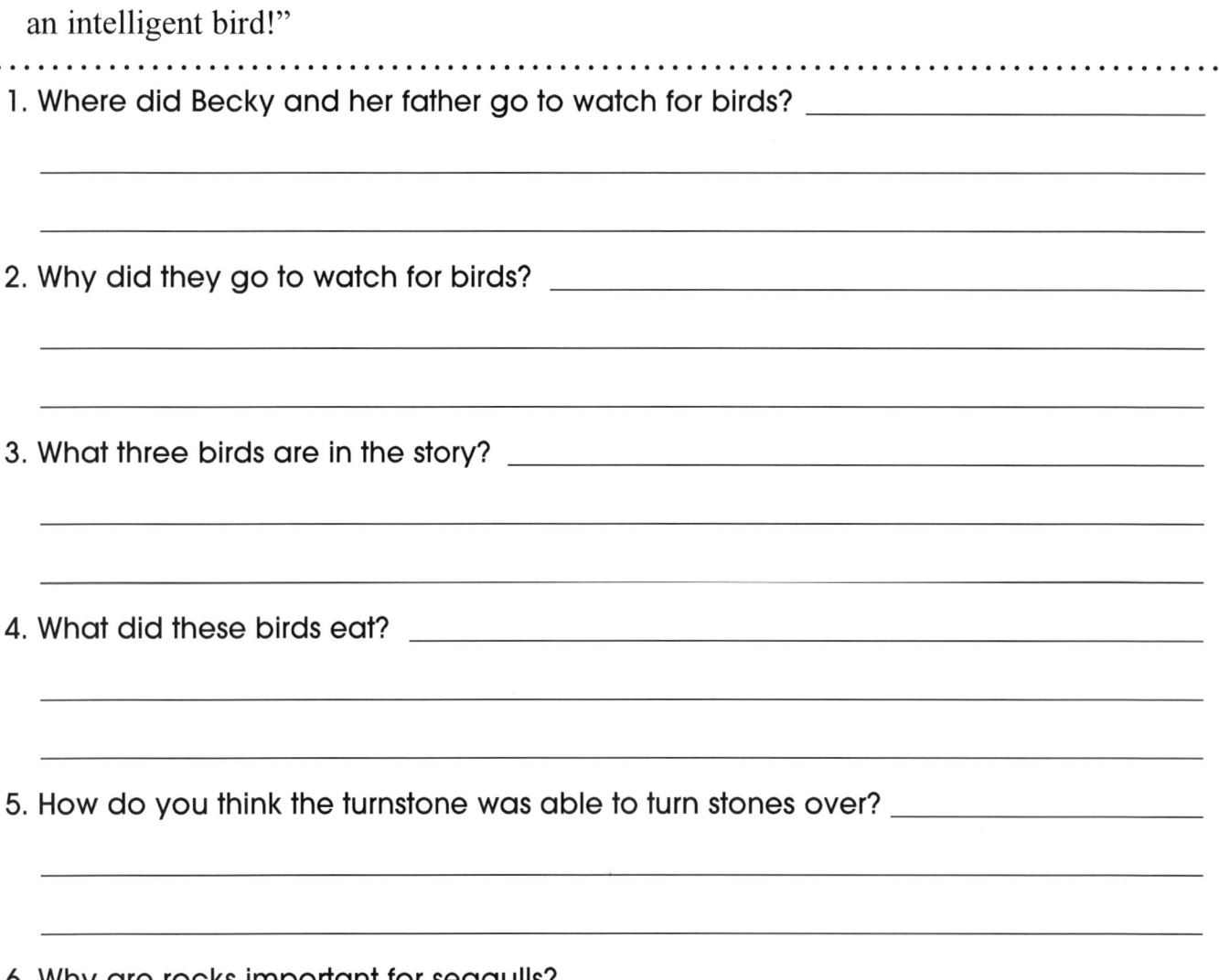

Then Father spotted a seagull flying by. The seagull dropped a clam onto a rock. The clam broke on the rock. The seagull flew down to eat the clam meat. Father said to Becky, "What an intelligent bird!"

1. Where did Becky and her father go to watch for birds? _____

_____

_____

2. Why did they go to watch for birds? _____

_____

_____

3. What three birds are in the story? _____

_____

_____

4. What did these birds eat? _____

_____

_____

5. How do you think the turnstone was able to turn stones over? _____

_____

_____

6. Why are rocks important for seagulls? _____

_____

Life in Alaska

The state of Alaska is very large. The number of wild animals in Alaska is a large number. Only a small number of people live in Alaska, though. Alaska is not an easy state in which to live. The winters in Alaska are long and cold. There is not much daylight in winter. Freezing temperatures keep most people indoors. Snow and frost and ice cover most of the land. Icy winds blow hard and strong.

The animals of Alaska do not mind the cold. A fish called *salmon* likes the cold rivers. Another animal that lives in Alaska's chilly rivers is the beaver. In the cold ocean, seals and walrus swim.

Other animals live in Alaska's forests. Bears hunt and sleep there. A large type of deer called *moose* live among the trees. Foxes and wolves and snowshoe rabbits dash through the woods, too. The animals of Alaska are wild and free.

· ·

1. Name nine animals that live in Alaska. _____

_____

_____

2. What two words describe Alaska's rivers? _____

_____

_____

3. Why do the fox and wolf and rabbit enjoy Alaska? _____

_____

_____

4. What does Alaska look like in the winter? _____

_____

_____

5. Would you want to live in Alaska? Why or why not? _____

_____

_____

Fun Things to Do

Another word for play is the word *recreation*. Recreation means activity that is done for fun. Recreation is a way to enjoy life. Some kinds of recreation are ways to relax. Reading is a relaxing recreation. Listening to music or going fishing is also recreation.

Some types of recreation are mental games. Mental games like card games are quite fun. Other fun games are board games and puzzles.

Another kind of recreation is sports. Sports are a recreation that many people enjoy. Sports are a kind of play and a way to enjoy life. Swimming is a fun recreation in the summer heat. Ice skating is a good recreation in the frosty winter. Baseball is a nice spring sport.

1. Why is reading a good recreation? _____

_____

_____

2. How are sports a way to enjoy life? _____

_____

_____

3. What three kinds of recreation are mostly about thinking? _____

_____

_____

4. Why is frosty weather good for ice skating? _____

_____

_____

5. Think of two other kinds of recreation for winter. _____

_____

_____

6. Why does music make a good recreation? _____

_____

TLC10588

Native American Art

Native Americans were the first people to live in America. They moved here more than 10,000 years ago! At that time, America was very natural. It was covered with plants, trees, and natural grasses. There were no streets, parking lots, or shopping malls. The Native Americans lived very well with nature. They used nature for all of their art.

Native Americans made wonderful art. Much of their art was handmade clothing. They actually wore their art! The Native Americans liked to make hats and bonnets from animal skins. They decorated the hats and bonnets with bird feathers. They made shirts and pants from the skin of deer. They cut buffalo skins to make heavy coats. The Native Americans were very artistic. Everything they used came from nature. They lived IN nature, and they lived WITH nature.

1. What was the Native American's whole life? _____

_____

_____

2. Why was their clothing a form of art? _____

_____

_____

3. Why were bird feathers important to Native Americans? _____

_____

_____

4. What animal skins gave them clothing? _____

_____

_____

5. Which animal skin was warmer? Why? _____

_____

_____

6. Why would Native Americans not want parking lots? _____

_____

Rainy Days

Troy was sick for a long time. For six weeks, he could not go to school. He could not exercise and he could not play. Troy sat in his wheelchair by the window. He loved to sit and wait for the rain.

When the rain came, Troy felt excited. He had a good view from the window. He could watch the raindrops falling. He could see big drops splash on the window. He could watch a bird take a shower in the rain. He could see a frog sit in a puddle of rain. He liked to see the wet rain dripping from the clouds.

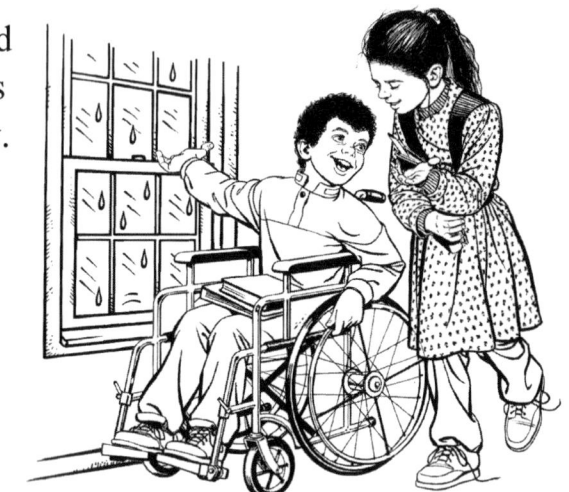

Troy had a plan. When he became well again, he would go outside in the rain. He wanted to stand in the rain. One day he would do that! He would feel the freshness of the rain on his skin.

. . . .

1. For what six things was Troy waiting? _____

_____

_____

2. Why was the wheelchair important for Troy? _____

_____

_____

3. Name four things the rain was doing. _____

_____

_____

4. Why does Troy dream of standing in the rain? _____

_____

_____

5. What else do you think Troy will do when he gets well? _____

_____

_____

Learning about Sand

Sand comes from rocks. Rocks break down because of the force of wind. Water also breaks down rocks. First, the rocks break into pieces called pebbles. Then the pebbles break into sand.

Sand sometimes moves through the air. It does that in a strong wind. A windstorm in the desert picks up a lot of sand. The wind carries the sand to new places. The sand will pile up into hills.

Sand also moves through streams and rivers. Sand tumbles in the water. The sand becomes smooth from tumbling and rolling on the water. That is what makes a sandy beach. The rolling of the ocean tides also smooth sand. Smooth sand makes a nice seashore. Remember that sand used to be a chunk of rock!

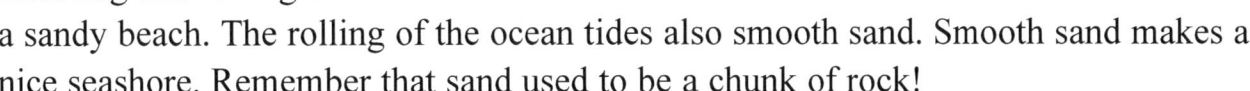

1. How do rocks break down? _____

_____

_____

2. From where do pebbles come? _____

_____

_____

3. Why is a windstorm in a desert very dangerous? _____

_____

_____

4. How could a traveler in a desert become confused about location?

_____

_____

5. What three things happen to sand in a river or stream? _____

_____

_____

6. Why is the seashore nice and smooth? _____

_____

The Smallest Continent

Australia is a small continent. It is the smallest continent on the planet! The land of Australia is mostly flat, like a large table. Some of this flat land is dry desert. Other flat parts are grasslands where cows and horses graze. Sheep also eat from these grasslands. The farmers and ranchers must protect their animals from the dingo. The dingo is a type of wild dog.

A few parts of Australia have mountains that are easy to climb. Some miners dig for gold and silver in the mountain rock. Other miners dig for a metal called copper.

Sometimes Australia does not get enough rain. In these dry areas, both the plants and animals thirst.

Thousands of wells go deep into the ground to bring up ground water.

1. What two kinds of flat land does Australia have? _____

_____

_____

2. About what two things do the farmers and ranchers mostly worry? _____

_____

_____

3. Why are the grasslands very important? _____

_____

_____

4. Why would miners want to go to the mountains? _____

_____

_____

5. How do people in the desert get enough water? _____

_____

_____

6. Why might it be easy to travel across the continent? _____

_____

North America

North America is a large piece of land. A big piece of land is called a *continent*. North America is a continent made up of more than one country. The three main countries are Canada, the United States, and Mexico.

Canada is far to the north. It is a country that has long and cold winters. Many wild animals live in the forests of Canada. Millions of fish swim in the cold lakes and streams.

The United States is also a part of North America. The United States is between Canada and Mexico. The United States has large cities and tall mountains. There is also the long Mississippi River.

Mexico is south of the United States and Canada. Mexico has beautiful, warm beaches for fun and play. Mexico is a hot country with a large, dry desert.

. . . .

1. On what continent do you live? _____

_____

_____

2. On what continent is Canada? _____

_____

_____

3. What country is between Canada and Mexico? _____

_____

_____

4. Where can a person catch food in Canada? _____

_____

_____

5. Why would a person in Canada like to travel to Mexico? _____

_____

_____

To a Flower

A hummingbird drinks with a sip.
She drinks with a tube, not a lip.
A hummingbird comes
To a flower and hums;
Then down the nectar she'll dip.

1. What words rhyme with "sip?" _____

_____

_____

2. Where does a hummingbird drink? _____

_____

_____

3. What does a hummingbird drink? _____

_____

_____

4. How does a hummingbird drink? _____

_____

_____

5. Copy this poem on your own paper.

6. Try to memorize this poem.

TLC10588

Types of Kites

Sally's dad loves kites. Sally's dad builds many kinds of kites. One day, he takes Sally to a museum in the city. There they see different styles of kites.

Sally and her dad spend two hours at the museum. They talk about each type of kite. There are 35 kites on display.

They see a regular kite. It is a flat kite made with two crossed sticks. This kite has a diamond shape. It is an easy kite to build. It is also quite easy to fly. But a flat kite is not strong. It might rip or tear in the wind.

Sally's dad shows her a box kite. A box kite is stronger than a flat kite. A box kite has many sticks for a frame. The frame holds two box shapes together. Both box shapes must balance. A person must be strong to fly a box kite.

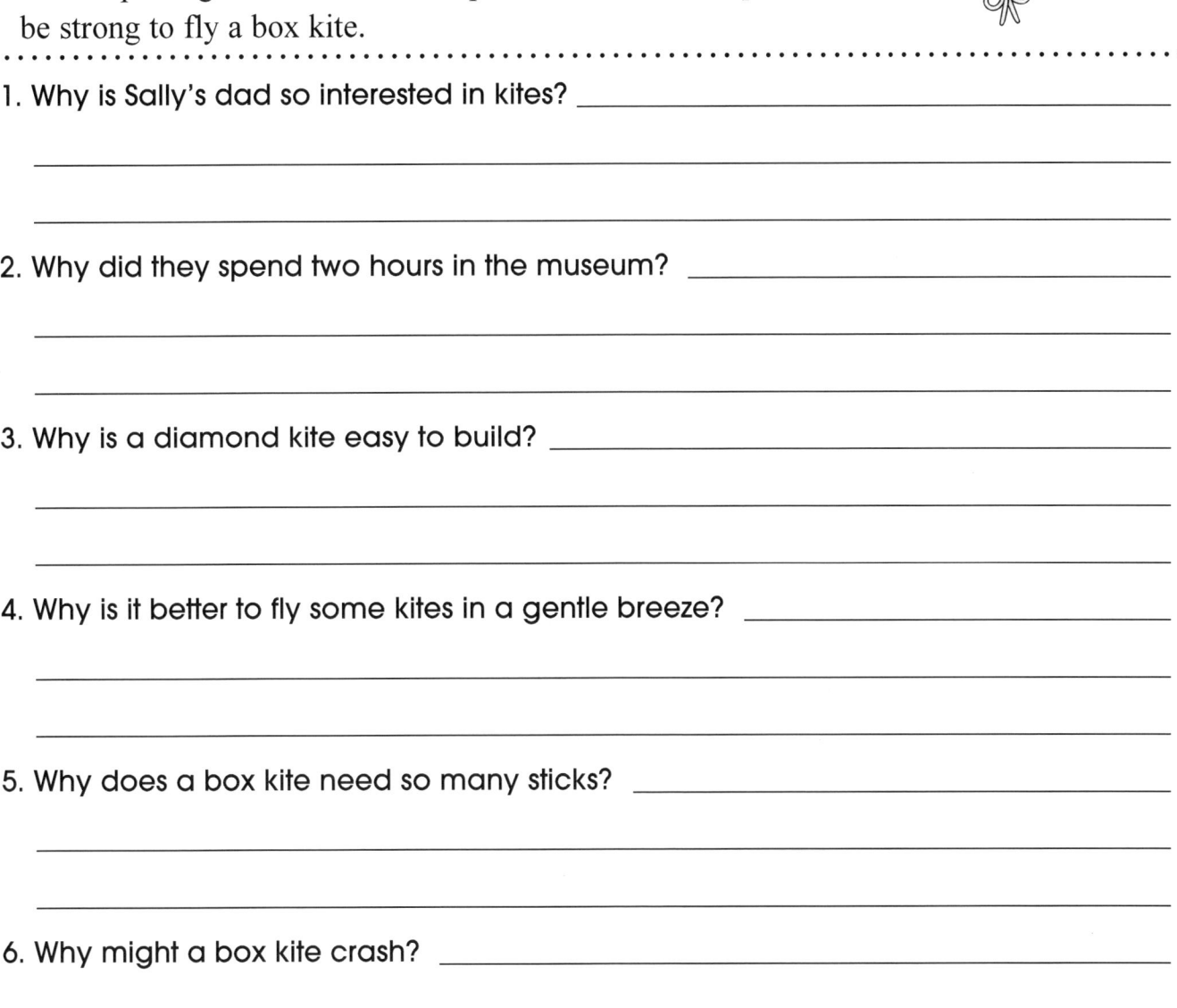

1. Why is Sally's dad so interested in kites? _____

_____

_____

2. Why did they spend two hours in the museum? _____

_____

_____

3. Why is a diamond kite easy to build? _____

_____

_____

4. Why is it better to fly some kites in a gentle breeze? _____

_____

_____

5. Why does a box kite need so many sticks? _____

_____

_____

6. Why might a box kite crash? _____

_____

Lots of Parrots

Not all parrots are large birds. One kind of parrot is small. It is called a *lovebird*. A lovebird usually stays close to its mate. Another small type of parrot is called a *parakeet*. A parakeet is most often a yellow-green color.

Very large parrots are often noisy. They might scream or squawk. They sometimes copy human words, too. These large parrots are strong. Their thick beaks are sharp like hooks.

One large parrot comes from the Amazon rain forest. This is a green bird with a bright yellow head. One large parrot from Africa is gray. A large red parrot lives in Mexico. This bird from Mexico is called a *macaw*.

1. What are three names for parrots in this story? _____

_____

_____

2. What is beautiful about most parrots? _____

_____

_____

3. Why do some people NOT like large parrots? _____

_____

_____

4. From where does the parrot with the least color come? _____

_____

_____

5. What three words describe a parrot's beak? _____

_____

_____

6. On your own paper, draw and color a picture of the parrot from the Amazon rain forest.

TLC10588

Feathers are Good

Have you ever found a feather on the ground? Sometimes, old feathers fall off the body of a bird. New feathers grow in the old feathers' places. Birds need many feathers to keep their bodies warm. The feathers also help the birds in flight. A few birds, like an ostrich, cannot fly.

People often pick up bird feathers from the ground. People use pretty feathers for many reasons. A pretty feather is a good way to decorate a hat. Very soft feathers are used to stuff pillows. Some quilts have soft feathers for stuffing. People might use bird feathers to decorate an art project. Some people put colorful feathers into a flower vase. A pretty feather is something to keep.

1. Why do birds need feathers? _____

_____

_____

2. Why don't birds worry if they lose their feathers? _____

_____

_____

3. What word in the story is like the word "fly?" _____

_____

_____

4. Find out why an ostrich cannot fly. _____

_____

_____

5. What are five ways that people use feathers? _____

_____

_____

6. On your own paper, draw a beautiful hat with feathers on it.

From a Bird Book

Teddy wanted to learn about birds. He asked his dad to help him. They went to the library to check out a bird book. That is how they learned a lot of facts about birds.

Teddy found out that a turkey makes a sound called a *gobble*. The sound of a goose is a *honk*. The noise from a duck is a *quack*. One kind of owl has a sound called a *hoot*. Another kind of owl says *poot*.

Teddy and his dad learned more about birds. They read about the roadrunner that runs on the ground. It almost never flies. Another bird is a cliff swallow that makes a nest out of sticky mud. A robin also makes a nest of mud. A robin eats worms from the mud. Teddy found out a lot about birds!

1. Did Teddy get a fiction or nonfiction book about birds? _____

_____

2. What is the information in a nonfiction book called? _____

_____

_____

3. About what seven birds did Teddy learn? _____

_____

_____

4. Why would rain be important for a cliff swallow? _____

_____

_____

5. Why would rain be important for a robin? _____

_____

_____

6. Which bird makes a sound like a car horn? _____

_____

_____

7. Which bird kicks up a lot of dust? _____

Leopards

Did you know that a cat can eat a dog? It's true! A leopard is a kind of large, wild cat. The favorite food of a leopard is dog meat. A leopard also hunts pigs, deer, and birds. A leopard is a fast and strong hunter.

Most leopards live in jungles, but some leopards live in dry deserts. In Africa, leopards live on grasslands or in hilly areas. Leopards run rapidly, climb tree trunks, and swim.

Most leopards have pale, yellow bodies with large black spots. Some leopards are all black. A panther is a kind of leopard. A leopard weighs less than a man, but the body of a leopard is eight feet long! A man is about six feet tall.

1. What four activities keep a leopard in good shape? _____

_____

_____

2. Name five places where leopards live. _____

_____

_____

3. Why do many animals fear the panther? _____

_____

_____

4. Why do some panthers live near a river? _____

_____

_____

5. What color of panther do you think is the most beautiful? _____

_____

_____

6. How do you know that some panthers do not need much water? _____

_____

_____

Earning Your Own Education

When you go to school, you are getting an *education*. Education is a way to learn new things. With an education, you begin to feel smarter and smarter.

Did you know you can also earn your own education? There are many ways to do this. Each day, when school is over, you can get more education. The best way to do that is to read. Reading many kinds of books gives you new information. That information is learning. You can learn about anything!

There are other ways to learn besides reading. You can listen to music after school. You can make extra sentences with your spelling words. You can look at maps and find places in the world. You can draw shapes on paper. These are ways to create your own education.

1. Why is education good for you? _____

_____

_____

2. Where do children get most of their education? _____

_____

_____

3. Name five ways you can get more education. _____

_____

_____

4. What is the very best way of getting extra education? _____

_____

_____

5. Why do you think music is good education? _____

_____

_____

6. How can you get education by using paper? _____

_____

What is a Brick?

Brick is a building material. A brick is rusty-red in color. A house can be made from many bricks. A fireplace and chimney are often made from bricks. Some people use bricks to cover a path or a street. Other people use bricks to build a garden wall.

Bricks are different from stones. Bricks are man-made. Stones are natural. A person makes bricks from mud. Each brick is in the shape of a rectangle. When each wet brick dries, it becomes very hard. Hard, dry bricks are good for building. Workers set bricks together with mortar. Mortar holds the bricks so they don't come apart. Something made from bricks looks beautiful.

. . . .

1. Why are bricks beautiful? _____

_____

_____

2. Why are bricks strong? _____

_____

_____

3. Why don't brick walls fall down? _____

_____

_____

4. Why is a brick wet at first? _____

_____

_____

5. Name six things that can be made from bricks. _____

_____

_____

6. Why do all bricks have the same shape? _____

_____

_____

Special Pants

Do you have a pair of jeans? Jeans are very special pants. People like them because they feel comfortable. People of all ages wear jeans. People wear jeans for fashion. Long ago, people wore jeans only for hard and dirty work. Jeans are still worn for work today. But now, jeans are also fashionable.

Children put on clean jeans with a nice sweater for school. Ladies wear jeans with fashionable boots for a party. Men put on a pair of jeans with a shirt and tie just for style. Jeans are popular. Some people sell their old jeans. Even jeans with scratches and tears are worn for style!

1. Why are jeans good for hard work? _____

_____

_____

2. Why are jeans good for fashion? _____

_____

_____

3. What clothing looks nice with jeans? _____

_____

_____

4. How can you tell old jeans from new jeans? _____

_____

_____

5. Why can people get money for old jeans? _____

_____

_____

6. Who do you think might never wear jeans? _____

_____

_____

TLC10588

Name _____

Sports Fans

Have you ever played on a sports team? Did anyone ever cheer for you? Did anyone want your side or team to win?

People who cheer for a team are called sports fans. Sports fans do not always go to the game. They often watch the game at home on TV. Sports fans might cheer for a basketball team. They might cheer for tennis players. They might want a favorite soccer team to win.

Not all sports fans cheer for a team. Sports fans sometimes just cheer for one player. Sports fans might shout for one swimmer. They might clap for one golfer. They might also have one runner for whom to root.

1. Where can sports fans cheer? _____

_____

_____

2. What are three words that mean "cheer" in this story? _____

_____

_____

3. Why do sports fans cheer? _____

_____

_____

4. For what three teams can they cheer? _____

_____

_____

5. What are some other team sports? _____

_____

_____

6. Why might people cheer for a swimmer? _____

_____

The Work of an Artist

An artist has a special talent. That talent is a special power. It is the power to create art. Art has a shape or design. It sometimes has color.

A painting on the wall is art. To make that painting, an artist used color. The artist chose the colors of paints to use. Then the artist used special brushes. With those brushes, the artist spread the paint. The artist made designs with the paint.

Another form of art is making vases or flower pots. An artist uses clay to make that vase or pot. The soft clay felt just right to the artist's hands. The artist smoothed the clay. Then they turned the clay on a special wheel. The wheel helped to shape the vase or pot. After that, heating and drying it was important.

1. What is an artist's power called? _____

_____

_____

2. What does an artist do with that talent? _____

_____

_____

3. How does an artist use paint? _____

_____

_____

4. What two things can an artist make from clay? _____

_____

_____

5. Why do artists enjoy using clay? _____

_____

_____

6. How does a clay pot become hard and strong? _____

_____

Postal Mail

Almost every day, mail comes to your home. This mail is delivered by a man or woman. This mail is not like email. This mail is called *postal* mail.

Postal mail might be a birthday card. It could be a letter or a paycheck. It might be a bill to pay. Postal mail comes in a closed envelope. In the top corner is a stamp.

The person who brings the mail is called a *mail carrier*. A mail carrier works hard to deliver the mail. Even if there is rain or a storm, a mail carrier brings the mail. When the weather is below zero, a mail carrier still works. A mail carrier even walks through deep snow.

. . . .

1. Who delivers the mail? _____

_____

_____

2. What four things might come in the mail? _____

_____

_____

3. Why do you think the envelope is important? _____

_____

_____

4. Why do you think envelopes need a stamp? _____

_____

_____

5. What does a mail carrier do in bad weather? _____

_____

_____

6. Name three ways postal mail is different from email. _____

_____

_____

Long Ago

A long time ago, America was very different. It was mostly farmland. Most Americans were farmers. Those farmers were called *pioneers*. They did not stay on one farm forever. Pioneers liked new adventures. They often moved their family farther west.

Pioneers did not have an easy life. It was difficult to find good land for farming. Sometimes the land would dry up. Sometimes too much rain would fall. Sometimes ice and snow would freeze the crops. But the pioneers did not give up. They started over in a new place. They found a path. They followed a trail. When they had trouble, they found a new place to live and tried again.

. . . .

1. Who were the pioneers? _____

_____

_____

2. Name three good adventures for the pioneers. _____

_____

_____

3. How did the pioneers know which way to go? _____

_____

_____

4. What were four weather problems the pioneers had? _____

_____

_____

5. For what three things were pioneers always looking? _____

_____

_____

6. How do you know they were brave? _____

_____

_____

TLC10588

Enjoying Nature

Tina and Rita are sisters. They have a favorite thing they like to do together. In the spring after the snow melts, they look for nature in their backyard.

Tina and Rita look around and collect a few things. Some things they NEVER take from nature. They never pick a green leaf from a tree. They know that a green leaf makes food and energy for the tree.

Tina and Rita also never take an insect that is alive. That is because a living insect will be food for another insect. Other animals eat insects, too. Tina and Rita have respect for nature. They know that nature is a world of beauty. They go to their backyard to discover our world. They look in wonder, and then they leave nature alone.

1. Why do you think spring is the girls' favorite season? _____

_____

_____

2. Name two places where the girls find a beautiful world. _____

_____

_____

3. Why don't they pick leaves from the trees? _____

_____

_____

4. Why do they leave insects alone? _____

_____

_____

5. Why do you think these girls respect each other? _____

_____

_____

6. Name three things you think they might collect and take in the house.

_____

_____

Small Houses

People live in all types of homes. Apartments are homes for many people. A farmhouse is another place to live. Some people live in a two-story house, but other houses are small. One small house is called a *cottage*.

Some people enjoy living in a cottage. It is easy to keep clean. A cottage is also cozy. That means everyone is in a small space together. A cottage is usually not fancy. Many people like to keep a cottage simple.

In some areas, people build a cottage near a lake. In other places, people live in a cottage by the sea. Other people have a cottage in the woods. A cottage might also be in a town.

. . . .

1. What are four kinds of homes in the story? _____

_____

_____

2. What four words describe a cottage? _____

_____

_____

3. How is a cottage different from a two-story house? _____

_____

_____

4. Where would a cottage have a natural view? _____

_____

_____

5. Why might a queen not want to live in a cottage? _____

_____

_____

6. How could you make a cottage fancier? _____

_____

TLC10588

Name _____

Animals Hide Away

Some animals hide in the winter. These animals *hibernate*. They cannot live in the snow because they can't stand the cold. They look for a warm place to sleep. They rest through the winter until spring comes.

One animal that hibernates is the bear. The bear hides away in a dark cave. It sleeps and rests and waits for the springtime. He snores deeply as he sleeps.

Many other animals hibernate. Turtles have their own shell in which to sleep. Frogs stay under the deep mud in the winter. Snakes hide in dark holes to hibernate. Insects hide under flat rocks. Lizards also escape the cold weather.

· ·

1. What does *hibernate* mean? _____

_____

_____

2. What six creatures in this story hibernate? _____

_____

_____

3. What are five actions of a hibernating bear? _____

_____

_____

4. When do snakes come out from their holes? _____

_____

_____

5. When do insects come out from the rocks? _____

_____

_____

6. Why don't we see frogs in the winter? _____

_____

_____

On the Farm

A farmer pays attention to the four seasons. The four seasons are important to a farmer. The weather of each season controls how a farmer works.

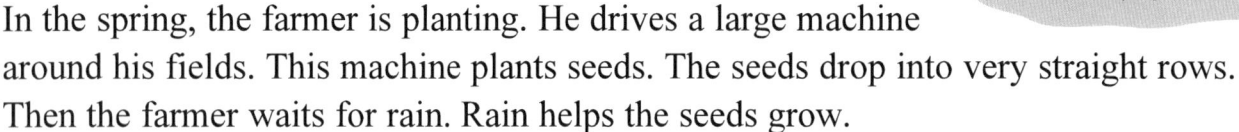

In the winter, a farmer's fields are resting. The fields rest under the snow. Cows and horses stay in the barn and chickens stay in their coop. Only the dogs run out in the snow.

In the spring, the farmer is planting. He drives a large machine around his fields. This machine plants seeds. The seeds drop into very straight rows. Then the farmer waits for rain. Rain helps the seeds grow.

In the summer, the hot sun gives heat. The farmer's fields need that heat. Heat is the power for the crops to grow. Rain clouds shower the fields with water.

Then the fall arrives. The crops are ready for picking. Apples and pumpkins are ripe. This is the time called *harvest*. The farmer has a lot of crops to sell.

. . . .

1. What season is busiest for a farmer? Why? _____

_____

_____

2. Why does a farmer have time to relax in the winter? _____

_____

_____

3. Why does a farmer's "new year" begin in the spring? _____

_____

_____

4. Name three reasons why summer is important to a farmer?

_____

_____

5. When does the harvest come? _____

_____

6. Choose one season on the farm to draw and color on your own paper.

Name _____

Non-fiction

So Many Ants

Ants are busy little insects. They always seem to be working. Ants rush to feed their colony. They are small, but they have a lot of speed. Their six tiny legs are very strong.

Ants run through the grass and the dirt. They climb up walls and fences. They work hard to build tunnels. They gather food.

Black ants can tickle a person's skin. They don't have a very bad bite. Red ants can attack a person. Red ants are small, but their bite is painful. Watch out for red ants when you sit on the ground!

. . . .

1. Why do ants have a lot of speed? _____

_____

_____

2. Name seven reasons why ants are so busy. _____

_____

_____

3. Where can you find ants? _____

_____

_____

4. How do ants bother people? _____

_____

_____

5. Which ants are the worst? Why? _____

_____

_____

6. Why do you think an ant colony is in a tunnel? _____

_____

_____

Staying in a Zoo

Out in the wild, animals have a lot of space. They can run and chase each other in a wild place. Wild animals have to run and chase to survive.

In a zoo, the animals settle down. They do not have much freedom, but they get a lot of care. In a zoo, the wild animals live quietly.

People protect animals in a zoo. The animals in a zoo do not live near their enemies. Some people work to feed the animals. Other people work as animal doctors. Some people take care of the newborn animals. Animals in a zoo are safe from many dangers.

. . . .

1. What are some wild places that animals might live? _____

_____

_____

2. Why do wild animals have a peaceful life in a zoo? _____

_____

_____

3. Do you think animals enjoy a peaceful life in a zoo? Explain. _____

_____

_____

4. What big danger don't the animals in a zoo face? _____

_____

_____

5. What wild instincts do you think zoo animals might keep? _____

_____

_____

6. Choose one zoo animal to draw and color on your own paper.

TLC10588

A Tall Stack

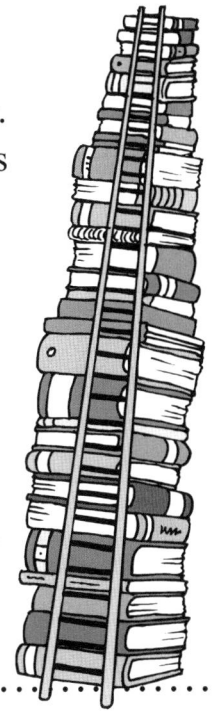

Vonnie keeps a tall stack of books. She reads before school each morning. Vonnie reads again when she gets home from school. Reading is Vonnie's way to learn about people and things. She also learns about our world.

Vonnie always has a book of poems in her stack. She learns about language this way. She also learns about words and rhyming.

Vonnie keeps books about pioneers in her stack. She reads about people from long ago. She knows a lot about American history. She thinks about the cowboys and farmers of the past.

At the top of the stack is a book of maps. This book is her atlas. Her atlas has maps of every country. She can find Japan in the atlas. She can also locate Denmark and New Zealand.

1. Why does Vonnie get up early each day? _____

_____

_____

2. About what four people does Vonnie read? _____

_____

_____

3. What three things does she learn from poems? _____

_____

_____

4. What book shows Vonnie the whole world? _____

_____

_____

5. Name three more countries. _____

_____

_____

7. Why does Vonnie learn so much? _____

_____

_____

How to Carry Things

Long ago, children did not use backpacks for school. Children used to carry their books in their hands. Some children used a little book bag. Others used a strap to hold their books together.

Long ago, people carried backpacks for sport. They carried things in a backpack to go camping. Sometimes climbers used backpacks to store gear while they climbed a mountain. Back then, people called their backpack a "rucksack." Hikers used a rucksack (or knapsack) to carry snacks. They would eat their snacks outdoors. They would stop hiking and eat in the woods or on the trail.

Children today put books and other things in a backpack. That makes a heavy backpack to carry to school!

1. What were old-style backpacks called? _____

_____

2. Who used backpacks long ago? _____

_____

_____

3. What do you think a camper put in his backpack? _____

_____

_____

4. Where did people carry their backpacks? _____

_____

_____

5. How did children used to carry books? _____

_____

_____

6. Name six things that children today put in a backpack for school.

_____

_____

_____

Puzzles

A puzzle is something that needs an answer. A puzzle really makes a person think. Some people do puzzles for their work. A police detective has to solve puzzles. A crime is a kind of puzzle. A detective uses clues to solve the crime.

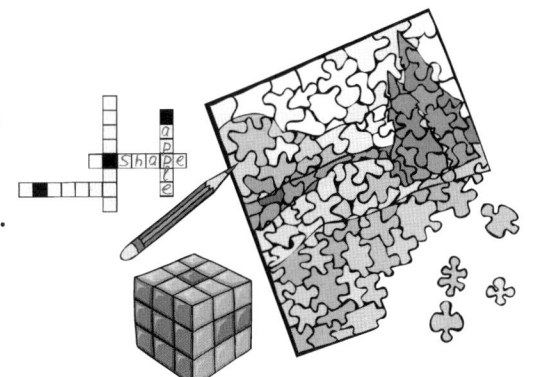

If you do crossword puzzles, you also use clues. You use clues to fill in the missing letters. Other people do jigsaw puzzles. They use clues of shape and color. They fit jigsaw pieces together. Some people do math puzzles. They have to follow clues about numbers.

Many things in nature are puzzles, too. Scientists try to find answers to puzzles about nature. How deep are the roots under a tree? That question is a sort of puzzle. Scientists search for answers to questions like that. They find clues in nature.

1. Name five different kinds of puzzles.

_____

_____

_____

2. Why is crime a puzzle for a detective? _____

_____

_____

3. How do jigsaw puzzles fit together? _____

_____

_____

4. How do scientists understand nature? _____

_____

_____

5. What puzzles have missing letters? _____

_____

6. Name three reasons why puzzles are good for the brain. _____

_____

_____

Many Lizards

A lizard is an interesting animal. It has cold blood. That is why a lizard likes sunshine. The bright sun warms a lizard's body. On cold, winter days a lizard hides away. It tries to find something warm.

More than 2,000 different kinds of lizards exist. Only two kinds are poisonous. One of them lives in the United States. It is called a *Gila monster*.

Many lizards are only three inches long. A gecko is a small lizard. It has sticky feet. That is why a gecko can run on walls and windows. A gecko can even run upside down on a ceiling!

Two kinds of lizards are called "dragons." One kind of dragon lizard is 8 or 9 feet long! Another dragon lizard is very small. It can actually fly by stretching out its skin to make wings!

1. Why do lizards hide in the winter? _____

_____

_____

2. Why aren't most lizards dangerous? _____

_____

_____

3. What is a Gila monster? _____

_____

4. Name two small lizards._____

_____

5. Onto what can a gecko stick? _____

_____

_____

6. Which dragon lizard would scare you the most? Why? _____

_____

_____

            TLC10588

Name _____

Our Sun

Our planet is part of a solar system. The word *solar* means "sun." The sun is in the middle of the solar system. Earth travels around the sun. Other planets, like Mars and Mercury, also go around the sun. Each planet goes around the sun in a loop called an *orbit*.

Our solar system has only one star. That star is our sun! Does it surprise you that the sun is a star? We see thousands of other stars in the sky. Those other stars are not in our solar system. Some of those other stars have their own planets. That makes another solar system.

1. What is our sun? _____

_____

_____

2. Can you name all the planets in our solar system? _____

_____

_____

3. Why do the planets go around the sun? _____

_____

_____

4. What path do planets take around the sun? _____

_____

_____

5. What star is in our solar system? _____

_____

_____

6. What objects are in any solar system? _____

_____

_____

Lindy's Dad

Lindy's dad is a baseball coach. He teaches his team how to play. He shows his players how to swing a bat. He teaches them to always play fair.

Lindy learns about sports from her dad. He wants her to know the rules of sports. He tells Lindy about golf. A golfer must be quiet on the putting greens. That is how a golfer is polite.

Lindy's dad tells her about Ping-Pong. A Ping-Pong player cannot double-bounce the ball. Next, Lindy learns about tennis. Her dad takes her to a tennis court. She learns why the lines on the court are important. The tennis ball must stay inside the lines.

1. Why does Lindy learn about sports? _____

_____

_____

2. What does the coach teach players about baseball? _____

_____

_____

3. What is important for a golfer? _____

_____

_____

4. Name one rule for Ping-Pong. _____

_____

_____

5. Why did Lindy's dad take her to a court? _____

_____

_____

6. Name three other sports you enjoy watching or playing.

_____

_____

Wild Animals of America

America has fifty states. Each state is quite different from the others. The animals of each state are different, too. Some animals in America are wild. Wild animals can be very dangerous.

The state of California has wild cats. These wild cats live in the high mountains. The wild cats are a kind of lion. They are called *mountain lions*. They are fast, strong, and fierce.

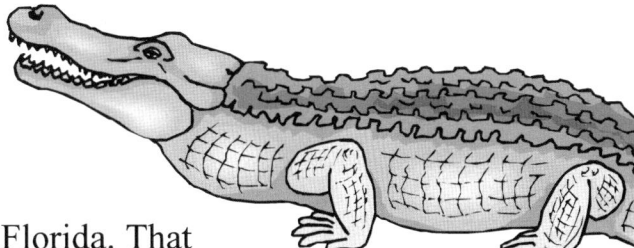

The state of Maine has moose. Moose are in the deer family, and they live in the wild. Moose are very large and have powerful bodies.

Another wild animal lives in the state of Florida. That animal is the alligator. The alligator swims and rests in the water. It attacks from the water. It moves fast and has a lot of strength.

1. Name three places where wild animals live. _____

_____

2. Name four wild animals that are in this story.

_____

_____

3. What wild animals are in your own state? _____

_____

_____

4. Write three words that describe a moose. _____

_____

5. Why are alligators dangerous? _____

_____

_____

6. Where do mountain lions live? _____

_____

_____

A Ladybird

A ladybird is not a bird at all. A ladybird is a bug! It is a ladybug! It is a very small beetle.

A ladybird has spots. Those spots are on the back of its shell. Many ladybugs are red and their spots are black. Other ladybugs have yellow or white spots. The female lays small yellow eggs.

In cold winter weather, ladybugs go under rocks. They stay warm under the rocks. When spring comes, the ladybugs are hungry. They fly away to gardens or fields to eat other insects.

1. What is a ladybird? _____

_____

_____

2. Why is the back of a ladybug special? _____

_____

_____

3. Why do you think the female's eggs are so small? _____

_____

_____

4. Why do ladybugs like springtime? _____

_____

_____

5. Where can a person find ladybugs? _____

_____

_____

6. Why are ladybugs good for a garden? _____

_____

_____

Wood for Building

Builders use wood to make houses. They use wood to construct schools. They build shops and restaurants from wood, too.

The wood people use to build things comes from trees. The wood is called *lumber*. Lumber is a flat board of wood. These flat boards must be very dry.

Lumber does not have any bark on it. Lumber is bare and smooth. Builders choose their lumber at a special store. They buy as many boards as they need. They also buy nails. They need enough nails to hold the building project together.

1. What two words in this story mean the same as *make*?

   _____

2. Name four things that are made from wood.

   _____

   _____

3. Think of three more things that are made from wood.

   _____

   _____

4. What is a flat, dry board called? _____

   _____

   _____

5. From where do we get lumber? _____

   _____

   _____

6. Why is lumber bare and smooth? _____

   _____

   _____

7. With what do builders build? _____

   _____

Writing on Paper

Some people use their computer for writing. They type reports and email messages. Typing a letter is also a way to write.

Writing on paper with a pen or pencil is also important. When you write with a pen or pencil, you do it by hand. That means you use your own handwriting. Each person's handwriting is special. To sign your name, you use your name or *signature*. Your signature is your handwriting, too.

Try to write by hand a letter on paper. Try to write a poem or story that way, too. Be sure to sign your name. Your signature makes that paper your very own. Your signature belongs only to you.

1. Name three ways people use a computer for writing.

   _____

   _____

2. Why do you think people like to use email? _____

   _____

   _____

3. What four things can a person write with a pen or pencil?

   _____

   _____

4. Think of two more things to write with a pen or pencil.

   _____

5. Why is writing with a pen or pencil important? _____

   _____

   _____

6. Why is a signature important? _____

   _____

   _____

Great Snacks

Muja's mom was busy peeling. She was peeling one orange fruit. She was peeling one orange vegetable. She was making Muja's snack.

The orange vegetable was a carrot. A carrot grows underground. It grows deep in the dirt. It is a healthy root. Muja's mom peeled the thin skin off the carrot. She washed the carrot and put it on Muja's plate.

The orange fruit was an orange. An orange grows on a branch of a tree. An orange begins as a tiny flower on the branch. That flower is called a *blossom*. The blossom turns into a fruit. Muja's mom peeled the thick skin off the orange. She sliced the orange for Muja. What colorful snacks Muja has!

1. What were Muja's two colorful, healthy snacks?

_____

2. Name four more healthy snacks._____

_____

_____

3. How do carrots grow? _____

_____

_____

4. What is an orange blossom? _____

_____

_____

5. Why do you think Muja didn't peel the snacks herself? _____

_____

_____

6. Why was the orange more difficult to peel? _____

_____

_____

7. Why was it important to wash the carrot? _____

_____

Reindeer

A reindeer is a large, strong deer. Its body and legs are very powerful. Each of its four strong feet is called a *hoof*. The reindeer can use a hoof to dig under the snow. The reindeer will do that to find food in the winter. In the spring and summer, the reindeer eats fresh grass.

A reindeer has horns on its head. The male and the female both have horns. These horns are called *antlers*. Antlers are sharp and pointy. A reindeer can fight with their antlers.

Reindeer live in cold places in the north. Because of this, they have thick skin. They have lots of hair on their skin. The hair is like a wool coat that keeps them warm!

1. What parts of the reindeer are very strong? _____

_____

_____

2. Where does the reindeer find food in the winter? _____

_____

_____

3. Which reindeer have antlers? _____

_____

_____

4. Why are the antlers good for fighting? _____

_____

_____

5. How do reindeer stay warm? _____

_____

_____

6. Find out in what countries reindeer live. _____

_____

_____

TLC10588

A Map of America

Open a map of North America. Find the fifty states. Remember that one of the states is a group of islands. Another state is north of Canada. Canada is not a part of America.

Locate the Mississippi River. It is many miles long. Find out how long it is.

Find the Gulf of Mexico. Imagine how deep it is. Imagine the powerful storms that sometimes happen there. Sometimes these storms are hurricanes.

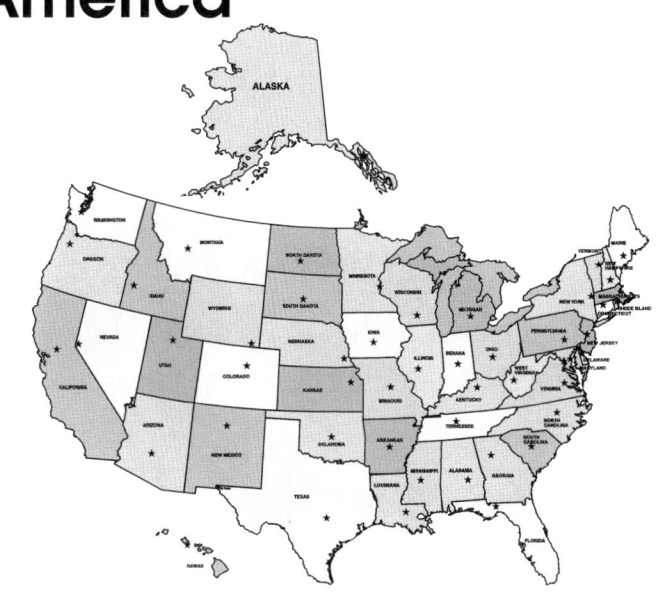

Look for the state of Washington. Then find Washington, D.C. They are on opposite sides of the country. Washington D.C. is not a state. It is a district. It is where the President lives. His family lives in the White House.

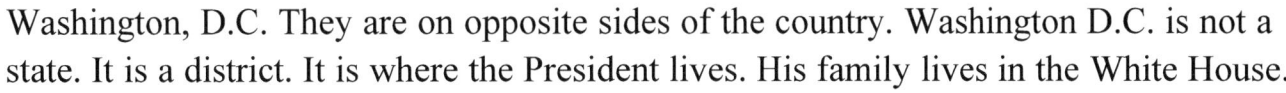

1. What is America's island state? _____

_____

2. What state is north of Canada? _____

_____

3. How long is the Mississippi River? _____

_____

4. Why is the Gulf of Mexico dangerous? _____

_____

_____

5. Where does our president live? _____

_____

6. Why is *White House* capitalized? _____

_____

_____

7. Make your own map of America on another piece of paper.

Where the Grass Grows

Some grass grows on farms. Cows eat that grass and so do horses. When the grass is dry, it is called *hay*. Cows and horses also eat hay.

Some grass grows very wild. Some grass grows as tall as a tree! This kind of grass is called *bamboo*. People use bamboo to make houses. They also use bamboo to make furniture.

In very cold places, grass does not grow well. This grass can be only one inch high. Some kinds of deer eat this grass. Reindeer and moose eat it, too.

1. What do cows and horses eat? _____

_____

_____

2. Name four animals that eat grass.

_____

_____

3. What is bamboo? _____

_____

4. How do you know bamboo is strong? _____

_____

5. Name two things that are compared to a tree in this story.

_____

_____

6. Why is some grass only one inch high? _____

_____

7. Draw a picture of an animal eating grass on your own paper.

     TLC10588

The South Pole

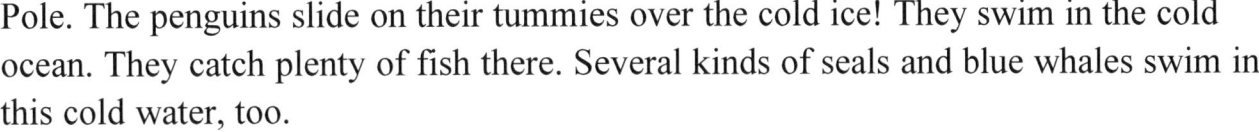

Most people will never travel to the South Pole. Only a few people have gone there. They went to the South Pole to study science.

The South Pole is a very special place. It is at the bottom of the earth. It has the coldest temperatures and the most ice. Ice is all around the South Pole. Beyond the ice is freezing ocean water.

Penguins live on the ice that surrounds the South Pole. The penguins slide on their tummies over the cold ice! They swim in the cold ocean. They catch plenty of fish there. Several kinds of seals and blue whales swim in this cold water, too.

....

1. Why don't most people go to the South Pole? _____

_____

_____

2. What could scientists study there? _____

_____

_____

3. Name three cold things that are at the South Pole.

_____

_____

4. Why do penguins like the South Pole area? _____

_____

_____

5. What is between the ocean and the South Pole? _____

_____

_____

6. On which continent is the South Pole? _____

_____

_____

A Map of the City

It is fun to study a map. A map has lots of information. You can learn many things. You can learn about places. You can learn about directions. A map also shows distance. You can find the distance from one place to another.

Open a city map. You will find city parks. You will see the city streets. You can see how to go north. You will find the way east. You can learn how many blocks it is to your school.

....

1. What three kinds of information are on a map?_____

_____

_____

2. Name three places can you find on a city map._____

_____

_____

3. What other places do you think you could you find on a city map?

_____

_____

4. What directions will you learn from a map? _____

_____

_____

5. What special distance can you find on a city map? _____

_____

6. Draw a map of your own neighborhood on another piece of paper.

Rain is Important

Some places get a lot of rain. Other places do not get enough. Deserts get only a little rain, while jungles get plenty.

Living things need rain. When rain falls, it fills the lakes. It also fills the rivers. Rain fills ponds and streams. That is how fish can live. That is where the bears get water to drink. Foxes drink there, too.

Falling rain goes into the ground. The ground soaks up the fresh rain. The roots of trees pull water from the ground. Trees grow tall from that water. Crops in farmers' fields also have roots. The roots of the crops pull up the water, too. Flowers in a garden get water the same way.

. . . .

1. Why doesn't a desert have lakes and ponds? _____

_____

_____

2. Name four places where bears and foxes go to drink.

_____

_____

3. Name four more animals that drink from those places.

_____

_____

4. How does the ground get enough water? _____

_____

_____

5. How do trees and crops get water to grow? _____

_____

_____

6. Why are roots important for flowers? _____

_____

_____

Where to Live

Some day, you will decide where to live. That is what grown-ups do. Adults often move to a new place. Some of them choose to live near the sea. Other grown-ups want to live in the desert.

To live near the sea is an adventure. The air has a very fresh smell. The wind is usually gentle. Sometimes a storm will come. Early in the mornings, fog is all around. The middle of the day has warm sunshine. That is when people swim and surf.

To live in the desert is an adventure, too! The air is hot and dry. There are almost never any clouds. Very little rain falls in the desert. The sun is very bright. People get a nice tan from the sun.

. . . .

1. Name two freedoms grown-ups have._____

_____

2. What other places do you think grown-ups might choose to live? _____

_____

_____

3. Why do some people live near the sea? _____

_____

_____

4. What are two problems of living near the sea?_____

_____

5. Why does the desert feel so dry? _____

_____

_____

6. Why do some people like the desert sun? _____

_____

TLC10588

The Force of Storms

Learning about storms and how strong they can be is an interesting science. Nobody can control a storm. Nature has all of the control. Humans can only wait for a storm to be over.

Some storms begin over the ocean. These storms are called *hurricanes*. Hurricanes create a lot of wind. They also produce a lot of rain.

Another kind of windstorm is a *tornado*. A tornado begins when cold air hits warm air. A tornado comes and goes suddenly. It is very strong and can sound like a train.

Another storm begins over the desert. This is a *sandstorm*. A very strong wind picks up the desert sand. The wind carries the sand in great clouds. The sand lands in a new place. People can lose their way in a sandstorm.

....

1. Why can't people control storms? _____

_____

_____

2. What are the three storms in the story?   _____

_____

_____

3. Why do hurricanes hold so much water? _____

_____

_____

4. Why do tornadoes sound like a train? _____

_____

_____

5. What two things will you find in a sandstorm?

_____

_____

6. Draw a picture of a storm on your own paper.

Clothes Washing

In most families, the grown-ups wash the clothing. They use a machine called a *washing machine* or *washer*. It is automatic, which means it runs by itself.

When a person turns on the washer, it fills up with water. After a person puts in dirty clothes, the washer is ready to work. The washer will shake the water around. The water will mix with soap. The soap and water will take off the dirt. Then the washer will rinse the dirt away.

A long time ago, people had no washers. They would just hit their clothing with a big heavy stick! That is how they would get the dirt out. Sometimes people would bang dirty clothing on a large rock. That was another way to get the clothes clean.

. . . .

1. What do people use today to clean their clothes? _____

   _____

   _____

2. What do you think *automatic* means? _____

   _____

   _____

3. Why doesn't a person have to fill the washing machine with water? _____

   _____

   _____

4. What does a washer need to work? _____

   _____

   _____

5. What does the washer do after it washes the clothes? _____

   _____

   _____

6. Why did pioneers have a hard time cleaning their clothes? _____

   _____

Surprises in the Forest

Just two miles from Keela's home is the forest. Keela's parents take her there. They go there to look for forest surprises.

Keela's mother drives the car. She parks the car where the forest trail begins. Keela and her parents stay together on the trail. They hike through the forest together. Keela cannot go alone.

Keela spots an old snakeskin. She thinks the snake has a new skin now. This old skin is thin and dry. Some ants are crawling into the snakeskin.

Then Keela sees some mushrooms. She cannot eat them! Some mushrooms are very bad. Behind one mushroom is a toad. The toad is brown and bumpy. It is not moving. It is just resting there. A ladybug runs past the toad. That surprised Keela, too!

1. What two things does the family do together? _____

_____

2. What five surprises does Keela find? _____

_____

_____

3. What two rules does Keela follow? _____

_____

_____

4. Why is the trail important in this story? _____

_____

_____

5. What sounds do you think Keela hears? _____

_____

_____

6. What else do you think she could she find in the forest? _____

_____

_____

Good Uses for Twigs

It is not only humans that use twigs. Some monkeys poke in the ground with twigs. That is the way they dig up something to eat.

People sometimes use twigs to draw a picture in the dirt. With a twig, a person could also write a message in the sand.

Some people use twigs for art or decoration. A lady might put twigs in a flower vase. A child could use twigs for a snowman's arms. Sometimes a grown-up puts marshmallows on a twig. That is a way to cook marshmallows over a campfire.

Twigs are useful tools!

. . . .

1. Who uses twigs? _____

_____

_____

2. Why do monkeys like twigs? _____

_____

_____

3. What kind of food do you think a monkey might dig up? _____

_____

_____

4. Why might a person use a twig at the beach? _____

_____

_____

5. What do you think is a danger of cooking with a twig? _____

_____

_____

6. Do you think twigs look good in a vase? Why or why not? _____

_____

_____

7. On your own paper, draw a snowman with twig arms.

TLC10588

Too Much Snow

Ned remembers last winter very well. Last winter, there was too much snow! The snow got in his way. There was so much snow, he couldn't even play.

The big snow was last January. Ned could not open his front door. He pushed and pushed the door. He slowly pushed away the snow. Then he climbed to the top of the snow pile. He slipped and fell. He got back up. Snow was in his boots. Snow was inside his mittens, too. Snow was even under his winter cap. Ned stood on the snow pile for a few minutes. Then he slid down to the bottom. He was ready to go back into his house.

· ·

1. In what season is January? _____

_____

2. What was Ned thinking about last January? _____

_____

_____

3. Why couldn't he hurry outside to play? _____

_____

_____

4. How do you know that Ned was strong? _____

_____

_____

5. Why did he get so cold? _____

_____

_____

6. How did Ned quickly get ready to go back into his house? _____

_____

_____

7. Write about your own snow adventure on another piece of paper.

After the Storm

Robbie wanted to play in his yard. His dad told him that he could not do that. His dad explained that the yard was a mess from the storm.

Robbie looked out the window. He saw what his dad meant. The storm had blown branches off the trees. Pine cones were all over the ground. The flower garden was muddy from the rain. The garden looked messy and pools of water were near the door. Twigs and sticks were everywhere. A strong wind was still blowing. Robbie's dad was right. This was no time to play outside.

. . . .

1. Why couldn't Robbie go outside? _____

_____

_____

2. Where did the storm cause a big mess? _____

_____

_____

3. What did the storm blow down from the trees? _____

_____

_____

4. What three problems did the rain cause? _____

_____

_____

5. What do you think will happen when the sun comes out? _____

_____

_____

6. On your own paper, make a picture of the yard after the storm.

TLC10588

Pennies

A penny is a small coin. It is not the smallest coin, however. A dime is smaller than a penny. A dime is worth ten cents, but a penny is only worth one cent! One cent does not buy very much. Grown-ups use pennies to help pay the tax on something they buy.

A penny is made from a metal called *copper*. Copper comes from the ground like other metals. It is the color of a penny. Copper is different from gold. It does not cost as much as gold. Copper is quite cheap, but it is very strong. It is good for making things besides pennies. Copper is used to make plates and pots, too.

. . . .

1. Name four things that are made from copper.

_____

_____

2. What is worth less than a dime? _____

_____

_____

3. What three coins are larger than a penny? _____

_____

4. Why aren't pennies made from gold? _____

_____

_____

5. How many pennies are equal to a quarter? _____

_____

_____

6. Which president's face is always on a penny? _____

_____

_____

Working in Space

Sam enjoys talking with his uncle. Sam tells his uncle about his dream. He talks about going to space when he grows up. He dreams of working in the space station.

Sam hopes to blast off in a rocket some day. That rocket will take him to the space station to work. He will be able see planet Earth from space. The space station will fly around Earth. Sam will sit at the windows of the space station. His job will be painting pictures of our planet!

1. What are Sam's dreams for the future? _____

_____

_____

2. Why is Sam's uncle important in this story? _____

_____

_____

3. Why will Sam have a great view of Earth some day? _____

_____

_____

4. What do you think Sam's paintings of Earth will look like? Why? _____

_____

_____

5. Do you want to travel to space? Explain. _____

_____

_____

6. What other dreams do you have? _____

_____

_____

_____

TLC10588

Design Work

Do you ever draw designs? It is fun to draw a design on paper. A design can be any shape you want. You can even design a completely new shape! That is why design work is creative.

Every object has a design. A toy has a design; so does a backpack. A jacket or a suit has a design, too. Another word for design is *style*.

Some people design furniture. A piece of furniture needs to be comfortable. A chair is designed for comfort. A sofa is styled for comfort, too. Even a mattress for a bed has a special style.

1. Where do you think all new designs begin? _____

_____

_____

2. Name things in this story that are designed. _____

_____

_____

3. What two words mean the same as *design*?

_____

_____

4. Why would a man want a suit with style? _____

_____

_____

5. Why is style important for furniture? _____

_____

6. On your own paper, draw a new design.

Nutrition

Nutrition is about the foods we eat. Good nutrition keeps our bodies healthy. With good nutrition, we can work, grow, and rest.

We get good nutrition from plants. Trees are one kind of plant. We get fruits like apples and pears from trees. We also get nutrition from small plants like rice and oats. From another small plant, we get wheat for our bread.

We also get nutrition from animals. If we eat hamburgers, we eat a meat called *beef*. Beef comes from a cow. When we eat bacon, we are eating pork. Pork is the meat of a pig. Butter is another animal food. How can that be true? Butter is made from fresh cream, and cream comes from a cow. Butter gives us nutrition, too.

1. Why is good nutrition important? _____

_____

_____

2. What five foods in this story come from plants? _____

_____

_____

3. Name four more plant foods. _____

_____

_____

4. Besides milk, name four things we get from cows.

_____

_____

5. What two things do you think are made from milk?

_____

6. What is bacon? _____

_____

_____

TLC10588

Animal Actions

A frog sometimes sits on a log.
A wolf can chase after a hog.
A bunny can leap,
A spider will creep,
And owls fly at night in the fog.

1. In this poem, what three words rhyme with each other?

   _____

   _____

2. Name two more words that rhyme with each other.

   _____

3. What are the six creatures named in this poem?

   _____

   _____

   _____

4. Why do owls need good eyes? _____

   _____

   _____

5. Copy this poem on your own paper.

6. Try to memorize this poem.

Name _____

Water Play

A shower feels good in the heat.
A rain shower makes a bird tweet.
A bug takes a bath,
Rain falls on the path,
And ducks splash along in wet feet.

· ·

1. What three words rhyme in this poem? _____

_____

_____

2. Name two more words that rhyme with each other._____

_____

3. What do you think *tweet* means? _____

_____

_____

4. Why do you think a rain shower make a bird tweet? _____

_____

_____

5. How do ducks use their wet feet? _____

_____

_____

6. Copy this poem on your own paper.

7. Try to memorize this poem.

A Sweet Treat

A cookie tastes good for a snack.

I have two or three in my sack.

I sit in the grass

With all of my class

And share my last cookie with Jack.

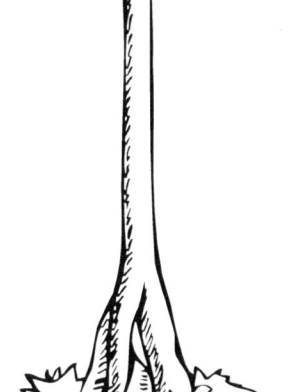

1. What three words rhyme with each other in this poem? _____

_____

_____

2. Name two more words that rhyme with each other. _____

_____

_____

3. Where does the class sit? _____

_____

_____

4. In this poem, where do you think the class went? _____

_____

_____

5. Copy this poem on your own paper.

6. Try to memorize this poem.

Coming Late

I sometimes arrive at school late.

That means that my teacher must wait.

She's tapping her toes,

She's blowing her nose.

But she smiles when I come through the gate.

1. What three words rhyme with each other in this poem?

   _____

   _____

2. Name two more words that rhyme with each other.

   _____

   _____

3. What are the four actions of the teacher?

   _____

   _____

   _____

   _____

4. When does the teacher relax? _____

   _____

   _____

5. Copy this poem on your own paper.

6. Try to memorize this poem.

TLC10588

The Dark Night

A storm came along in the night.

The thunder did give me a fright.

I heard a dog bark,

Awake in the dark,

Then something sure made the room bright!

. . . .

1. What three words rhyme with each other in this poem? _____

_____

_____

2. Name two more words that rhyme with each other.

_____

_____

3. What were the two sounds in this poem?

_____

_____

4. What do you think made the room bright? _____

_____

_____

5. Copy this poem on your own paper.

6. Try to memorize this poem.

Grapes

A grape does not grow by itself. It grows in a bunch with many other grapes. That bunch is called a *cluster*. Many clusters of grapes grow on a long vine. The vine must be strong. The vine holds the weight of a lot of grapes!

Grapes taste juicy and sweet. Grapes have a lot of liquid. That is why grapes make a good fruit drink. Did you know that grapes can also be made into wine?

Do you ever eat raisins? Raisins are actually grapes! Raisins are grapes that have dried out. The hot sun dries the juice from the grapes. The grapes shrink into little raisins.

1. What grows on a grape vine? _____

_____

_____

2. How can a grapevine hold so many grapes? _____

_____

_____

3. Name three reasons why grapes make a good fruit drink.

_____

_____

_____

4. Why is a raisin a fruit? _____

_____

_____

5. What happens when grapes dry out? _____

_____

_____

6. On your own paper, draw bunches of grapes on a vine.

has completed the

assignments and is an official

Reading Master!

_____ certifies that

_____

has some awesome

Reading
Power!

Super Reader Award

Presented to _____

by _____

Super Reader Certificate

Presented to _____

by _____

for outstanding work!